How Not
to Kill Your
Houseplants

How <u>Not</u> to Kill Your Houseplants

The Foolproof Guide to Lush, Healthy Plants

BY ANN PREGOSIN

Color photographs by David Pregosin
Line drawings by Mona Mark

COLLIER BOOKS
Macmillan Publishing Company / New York

Macmillan Publishing Company
866 Third Avenue, New York, N.Y. 10022
Collier Macmillan Canada, Inc.

Library of Congress Cataloging-in-Publication Data
Pregosin, Ann.
  How not to kill your houseplants.
  Includes index.
  1. House plants.   2. Indoor gardening.   I. Title.
SB419.P74   1986   635.9'65   85-31372
ISBN 0-02-081180-2 (pbk.)

Macmillan books are available at special discounts
for bulk purchases for sales promotions, premiums,
fund-raising, or educational use. For details, contact:

Special Sales Director
Macmillan Publishing Company
866 Third Avenue
New York, N.Y. 10022
            10 9 8 7 6 5 4 3 2 1

DESIGNED BY MARY CREGAN
PRINTED IN THE UNITED STATES OF AMERICA

For Lexie

Contents

Acknowledgments

Just like a plant, a book doesn't spring into existence and go forth to develop and blossom all on its own. It needs inspiration to get off the ground, it needs nurturing to keep it going, it needs good editing to separate the wheat from the chaff, and it needs coordinated effort to keep all parts pointed in the right direction.

I am indebted to several persons whose support and talents greatly influenced every phase of this work. Foremost is my husband, David, who singlehandedly took on most of the responsibilities of business and home, in order that I could devote my time and energies to the writing of this book. Far from collapsing under the weight of double-duty, David persevered with typical tenacity and deeply appreciated good spirit and humor.

A strong belief in one's literary talents comes hard. It improves considerably when a talented, highly successful literary agent takes you under her wing. A few years ago, Elizabeth Knappman took me under her wing. She encouraged me, she helped develop the concepts for this work; then, with equal finesse, she took this book to the marketplace.

"What's in a name?" The *right* title conveys a book's import and tone. From the head of our dear friend, Andrew Deutsch, sprang the title for this work. Thanks again, Andrew!

Does an editor make a difference to a book? A good editor makes *all* the difference. In writing this book, I was blessed with a *great* editor, Alexia Dorszynski. She and her expert associate editor, Jill Herbers, could not have been more helpful, more astute, or more dedicated. These two ladies could edit a book in a foreign language and still get it right!

Last, I want to acknowledge the longtime friends and ever-faithful customers of The Village Green Garden Shop in Park Slope, Brooklyn, New York, whose questions and concerns and love for their houseplants inspired the need for this work. This book is written for each and every one of you.

Ann Pregosin
October 1985

The Village Green Garden Shop
814 Union Street
Brooklyn, New York 11215

How <u>Not</u>
to Kill Your
Houseplants

1.

How <u>Not</u> to Go Out Looking for Disaster

(And Pay Good Money for the Experience) *or* Where <u>Not</u> to Buy Your Plants

What's wrong with the plant in photograph 8 of this book?

While you're thinking about that, also ask yourself: Does the condition of this plant look familiar? Does it ring a little bell of recognition? Or is it more like a loud siren? As you can plainly see, this is no Alice in Wonderland plant. Nor is it one of the plants that adorn the pages of your other plant books—those robustly healthy ones that practically leap off the page right into your lap! Good Lord, no!

Let's see if we can't muster our courage and take a closer look at our very down-to-earth, unhappy plant. To benefit fully from this experience, you must take in every telltale detail, every sign, every nuance, every *shade* of this plant's major discontent. Let's start with an overall appraisal. Scan the general weakness of this plant. Note how limp, skimpy, and flimsy it is. It looks tired, debilitated, and exhausted. It's messy and depressing. It's the kind of look you want to throw a paper bag over,

should guests with normal vision arrive at the door unexpectedly.

Now let's move in for an even closer look. Turn up
the lights if you need to and carefully observe all those
blank spaces where leaves have fallen off. What's the
fate of the remaining leaves? It's not exactly promising.
Half of them are already yellowing and browning, and
the rest look as though their green days are numbered.

Not a pretty sight, is it? But then, this is not a pretty
story. Now we want you to go a step further and try to
imagine the consistency of those limp leaves. Does a
lump of overcooked spinach come to mind? If it does,
you're on the right track. Those leaves are soggy, waterlogged.

All things considered, one could safely say that here,
before our very eyes, is a portrait of a plant *on its way
out*. But you probably don't need the grim visual aid of
our miserable specimen hanging in there by a root or
two, with a few paltry leaves here and there to wrap
around itself. Why not? Because you already have one
of your very own sitting not three feet away from you.
Or maybe you have two? Or three? Is it possible that
we're talking about your whole collection of plants?

Don't get all upset at this point. Let us assure you
that you're in the best of company. Every year we deal
with hundreds, perhaps thousands of nice folks just like
yourself who are sitting across the room from some miserable, halfhearted, half-*dead*, half-green pet whose
prognosis is just as bleak as the specimen in photograph
8. Just as we turned those plant lovers and the fate of
their wards around, so also will we reform you and your
plants.

Let's jump right in now and start the upward and

onward process that will put those elusive green gods in *your* corner too. Is it painful? Not at all! Will it work? Absolutely! Your diploma will be something you never had before: a bona fide green thumb.

With this positive attitude in place, let's go back to our victim in the pot and start at the beginning, with what went wrong with this plant. Where *is* the beginning? It's not the fact that this plant needed bright light when all you had to offer was shade. It's not the fact that it had a case of spider mites to begin with. It's not that its soil is packed down like a brick. Nor is it that you overwatered and then underwatered. It's not that it was denied fertilizer when it was trying to grow and then overfertilized when it was trying to rest. Nor is it that it was transplanted when it should have been left alone. It's not even that the kitty mistook the pot for her litter box and left a little present, adding insult to massive injury. No. While any one of these events alone is serious enough to turn the tide against any plant trying to make it in this world, none of these events is the beginning. What went wrong with this plant starts with *where* it was purchased.

If we can borrow the design of a baseball diamond, the plant source is "home plate." To get anywhere else, a baseball player has to start here. However impressive his other talents, if he strikes out at home plate, he will never have a chance to go to "first base," much less "second" or "third." And forget about a "home run." The player's ability to run the bases starts with his performance at home plate. In the same way, your ability to grow plants starts at home plate: *their source.* It starts with the *plant dealer* who is selling them, *how* he is selling them, and the *condition* of the plants. If you are ill-informed, get careless, get lazy, look for shortcuts, or get taken in by "prices too good to be true," you and your plants will never get off the ground. Like the base runner, you strike out at home plate. You blow it before you even begin!

So fasten your seatbelts. We're about to take a little tour of where *not* to buy your plants. While we're at it, we're going to explode some old myths about plant sources that have not only been keeping the green revolution down but have been keeping it a definite brown. We term these locations on the map "Guaranteed Misery Sources." They're guaranteed to cause misery and disappointment, and will waste your hard-earned money. So climb aboard, and here goes!

Guaranteed Misery Source Number One: The Supermarket. You've been there a thousand times. You'll go back a thousand times more. With the tunes of Muzak in the air presumably to put us in the mood, there is aisle upon aisle of every household good. Typically, somewhere between fruits and vegetables lurks the "Plant Department."

The plant department can feature rows of plants lined up like so many boxes of bathroom bowl cleaner, or it can be free-form clusters of pots rudely thrown together like a bunch of overripe cantaloupes on special. Then again, sometimes the frozen food department is the plant department. Here half-frozen green specimens are huddled together on top of freezer units, and frigid air is blasting on tropical plants as though they were a colony of penguins. But this "big chill" is, unfortunately, only one part of the factory treatment that innocent plants receive at the corner supermarket.

Take maintenance. That seventeen-year-old pimply kid who has been assigned to restack the apple and orange bins and give the wilting parsley a daily spritz is the same kid who gives the rubber trees a daily dousing. No matter that the soil is already saturated (and has been since the trees were unloaded off a dark, dank truck two weeks ago). They told him, "Soak 'em every day, Sam." That's exactly what Sam does. No matter that from day one leaves have been turning yellow and falling off from (would you believe?) overwatering. Sam figures they really must be thirsty if they're turning yellow and sometimes douses these trees *twice* a day. To this very same miserable row of overwatered, waterlogged, water-soaked rubber trees daily march troops of customers only too happy to plunk down the $20. Then they take home a potful of misery.

If you're getting depressed, you should. Now we're about to go from bad to much worse. This horror is called Holiday Plant Time at the Supermarket. It's also called Clear Out All the Dead Mums Still Stuck in Their Suffocating Plastic Wraps That Never Sold for Thanksgiving (despite the advertised rock-bottom price), and Bring On the Legions of Poinsettias for Christmas. Load up the frozen food department. Throw 'em in with the fruits and vegetables. *Stuff 'em in anywhere they'll fit.* Slap on a "dirt cheap" price. Then advertise them on TV with the Butterball turkeys as "ready to make your holidays glow."

If you're normally prone to the "holiday blues," you'd better look the other way when it comes to a closer inspection of all this cheer in a pot. There are few things sadder in the plant world than the sight of these mass-produced, sloppy, frail, miserable, grade Z poinsettias.

From the greenhouse to your holiday table they are neither produced, handled, nor sold with even the same
care the Styrofoam industry allots its cups. Speaking of
supermarket plants and Styrofoam cups, they curiously
and sadly have one thing very much in common—they're
"throwaways." Each comes with a built-in death-
replacement factor.

How's that? The holiday poinsettias, the massive Easter
lily invasion that will follow in the spring, and most of
the everyday plants you find languishing in the supermarkets are not expected or intended to survive by anyone except you, the retail buyer! *Everyone else knows the
score.*

What's the score? The vast majority of plants that end
up on your supermarket's shelves are mass-produced
in huge greenhouse compounds all across the nation.
The idea is to grow them up fast with sleek conveyor-
belt efficiency and ship them out even faster to meet the
huge quotas of the supermarket chains. Forget about
quality; the god here is quantity. The result is under-
sized, underrooted, overfertilized but still undernour-
ished, low-grade plants rushed up through the system.
They will eventually be unloaded at your local market
with all the tender loving care reserved for throwing
around sacks of potatoes.

Once in the store, they come under the jurisdiction
of our renowned horticulturist with vegetable experience, Sam, the Watering Can Kid. Sam sweeps the floors,
lines up the tomatoes, flirts with the girls. He also waters
the plants and hauls out the dead ones every two weeks.
Even if he did care more about plants, *he knows less.* So
if the name of this brutal game is Survival and the con-
tenders are the Styrofoam cup and a supermarket plant,
you'd better put your money on the cup.

"Throwaway" plants? We think so. We wouldn't be surprised if we were talking 99 percent mortality. The only practice across our land that rivals this veritable slaughter-for-profit is the industry that produces the baby chicks one sees in pet shop windows at Easter time. They are 100 percent doomed. Here there are virtually no survivors. Why? In both instances the mentality behind production, distribution, and sale is the same. The practices are the same. The total disregard for life is the same.

So when you go to the supermarket tomorrow, take a new look at that plant department. At the checkout line, check out the plant helplessly rolling around in the cart behind yours. Take an even better look, if you dare, at the dying plant in the cracked pot already discarded behind the rack of *TV Guides*. This one never even made it out of the store. Then you decide. By the way, allow us to point out that your local five-and-dime store is nothing less than an identical twin in its acquisition and treatment of plants for sale. The only difference is that here we have a kid named Cliff in charge of watering.

Next, we're going to take a little walk around the corner from the supermarket to take a look at *Guaranteed Misery Source Number Two: The Street Vendor of Plants*. In areas where they're not prohibited by law (and in many where they are!) warm weather brings out these vendors like a plague of aphids headed for your annuals. The operation can be as simple as the guy in a station wagon across the street from the gas station who unloads two dozen plants. The more organized vendors get it together enough to haul in a small truckload replete with shelves, folding chair, and an umbrella. They wait there like patient spiders for their unknowing victim: you, the public. Half the time they have no permit to sell anything. They're not certified by the Department of Agriculture. They're licensed and regulated by no one. But what they *do* have is the desire to make a buck and to unload their goods on you. This week it's plants. Next week it's watermelons. It's all the same. Like the buyers for supermarkets and five-and-dimes, this guy uses plant growers and distributors who specialize in cheap, high-production plant crops with little or no regard for quality. He buys up a bunch, hauls the load back to the street corner, throws up a scribbled sign that reads BARGAIN PLANTS, and waits for you to show up. And you show up by the thousands!

This guy is no fool. He knows what he's doing. He maintains no regular hours, has no overhead, and pays no rent, insurance, electricity, salaries, or taxes. But he knows how to hook you. He wants you to believe that his plants are the same as the plants that are sold in the garden shop down the street for five dollars more. Then, with a sweep of his magic marker, he's ready to "knock off a little something more" or sell you at rock-bottom prices not one but two of his bug-infested, yellow-leafed, prized plants that a reputable dealer wouldn't even think of grinding up for fertilizer.

A week later, your plants are really looking awful. Somewhere in the back of your mind you have this sneaking suspicion that you just might have been taken. You return to the street corner to have a word with our friend relaxing under the umbrella. Lo and behold, he's gone! There you are standing on the street corner in the hot sun with your bag of yellow leaves. You have absolutely no recourse. Meanwhile, our dealer collected his shelves, threw the rest of his junk (plants included) into the truck, grabbed the umbrella and chair, and fled. This guy is already exploiting greener pastures. Oh, yes. There's just one more thing he has with him: *your money*.

Think you've had enough? Do you get the picture yet? For those of you who still believe there's any kind of bargain out there on the streets, we're going to make yet another stop. Again, it's a familiar one. This time you may have to hop in the car to take a short ride to *Guaranteed Misery Source Number Three: The Flea Market*.

The flea market dealer of plants has much in common with the guy on the street, with the possible exception that this venture is a little more organized. Unlike the guy on the street who is as free as the air, the flea market dealer actually pays a little overhead, like rent, however nominal, and perhaps a share of other expenses such as electricity. But we assure you that, where you're concerned, the deal is the same. Last year this guy sold brass candlesticks, but they didn't go so well. This year he thought he'd try plants. So he goes to those same brokers frequented by the street vendors and five-and-dime and supermarket chain buyers to haggle over that same grade F material a reputable garden shop wouldn't want to *give* away. This low-grade stock is interchangeable. The misery you will experience struggling with these plants is also interchangeable.

Yes, it's true that the guy at the flea market won't exactly be skipping town when you go back and try to discuss what happened with your plants. But the problem is, the guy may have no idea he sold you junk because he knows nothing about plants (which doesn't help you). Or, much worse, he does know he's dealing in throwaway junk. As you try to ask legitimate questions, you'll be rebuked so rudely by this illegitimate dealer that you'll be happy to get out of the place alive. In any event, our dealer isn't worried. He knows that if his plants don't move this year, he can always sell "sneaker seconds" next year.

We're sorry to say that this journey, which always ends in hardship for you, isn't quite over yet. But take heart, because we're in the homestretch now. There is only one last obstacle in our way, and that is *Guaranteed Misery Source Number Four: Sales That Feature Plants Already Half-Dead*. These sales occur in not-so-reputable plant stores, garden centers, florists, department stores, and conceivably anywhere else plants are sold. But wherever they occur, carefully note that there is a big difference between a sale that features plants already half-dead and a "clearance sale." One is an obnoxious ripoff; the other is a perfectly legitimate, normal business practice that a dealer resorts to when overstocked with a particular plant or when the space is simply needed for another purpose. Here there's no pressure, no hard sale, no strong-arm tactics, no reject plants at phony bargain rates. There are no losers in this transaction, only winners.

Sales that feature plants already half-dead, however, are an entirely different matter. Here plants are being offered at a "reduced" rate because the plants *themselves* are reduced. They've dropped leaves. Stems have rotted out. Loads of discolored leaves had to be pruned off. In short, they're a mess. Into this collection of unfortunate plants, our disreputable dealer now sticks his sign reading TUESDAY'S SPECIAL. Well, that sign should really read TUESDAY'S RIPOFF because that is exactly what it is. You have about as much chance of success with these ripoff plants as you have with the plants sold in the supermarkets and five-and-dimes, and those hawked by the vendors. *Maybe,* with expert tender loving care, one-tenth of these debilitated plants *might* be revived to go on to lead normal lives. But the forecast is bleak because only a skilled eye is going to recognize a good candidate for rehabilitation. And then only someone with considerable experience will know how to bring such a plant back from the brink. The analogy is: With a good eye and expertise you can weed out the obscure designer garment in a "last chance" bin in the bargain basement of a department store. But do you *really* want your success with plants to hinge on the slim odds of weeding out that one gem?

Use your head! If the price on a plant (wherever it comes from!) looks too good to be true, chances are it is! Plants are no exception to that sturdy old adage that in this world you get what you pay for. You don't buy a television from a cheese store, so don't buy your plants from a man who's really more into watermelons. If you want to know something about the plants you are buying, do yourself a real favor: From this moment on, go to a decent dealer who cares and knows something about the plants he is selling.

Who or what is a decent dealer? It's the fellow or gal who specializes in and works with plants seven days a week, fifty-two weeks a year, year in and year out, who has made the commitment to and major investment in a permanent business. He or she must succeed in providing quality plants, quality service, and quality advice over and over again. This person is none other than the proprietor of your local plant shop, garden center, or florist. The fate of this person's business depends upon your patronage. But, we assure you, your fate and the fate of your plants *start* with him. So *use* him!

Now let's say you swear off each and every one of the aforementioned "guaranteed misery sources" as places to buy your plants. You take our advice and head straight for that wonderful plant shop down the street. And you're quick to admit that it's such a relief to be able to shop for plants without dodging cars in the street or hearing the monotonous drone of Musak in your ears, the screeching of bratty kids at the five-and-dime, or the barking voices assaulting your senses at flea market plant stands. Finally! You know you're pointed in the right direction. You're standing in the doorway of a bona fide plant shop, an enterprise whose *raison d'être*, whose sole purpose, is to sell plants and provide expert care.

You're itching to buy something, so you cross the threshold. Your attention is immediately caught by a display of foliage plants. You pick one up and hold it. "This looks good," you think. But you put it back when a flowering plant a little further in catches your eye. You proceed to examine this one and its extraordinary blossoms. "Wouldn't it be nice to have something with color?" you think. But this one, too, you quickly return to the display. "What's the matter?" you ask yourself. What is this uneasy feeling tugging away at the pleasure of finally being surrounded by all these wonderful plants? "I paid my dues," you reassure yourself. "I made the flea market and supermarket rounds. I paid for those mistakes in every way. Now I know better. But why don't I *feel* better?"

Yes, you kicked the insidious flea market plant habit. Yes, now you buy only your food and household goods at the supermarket. But having turned your back on those "guaranteed plant misery sources," did you think that merely placing yourself in a plant shop would guarantee you an instant ticket to the glories of the Plant Kingdom? Did you think you would be graced with a Hereafter lined with heavenly green celestial bodies there for the taking? Or a "Paradise Found" just waiting to be plucked? Not so.

What's missing in this should-be-happy picture is *confidence*. You have none and you know it. *You don't know how to shop for plants.*

Well, cheer up! Not only is this admission of a very common affliction not a cause for gloom, it is cause for celebration. Having isolated what is holding you back from freely partaking of the joys of new plant buying, we can do something about it. We can begin to cast off that insecurity and start the process that will turn you into a full-fledged sharp shopper. Just as Ralph Nader is only too happy to point out the pitfalls and lemons in the shiny new-car lot, so are we ready to guide and teach you what to avoid in even the nicest plant shop, garden center, and florist.

So let's tour that plant shop together. Let's start the overall appraisal with the following: Just as a healthy-looking person tends to be healthy, generally speaking, in the plant world *what looks good* is *good*. For instance, in what manner are plants displayed? Whether they're lined up like soldiers or artfully clustered together, you don't want to see the kind of crowding that will cause tattered and broken leaves. You saw enough of that plants-packed-in-like-sardines treatment in the supermarket to last a lifetime. After all, *someone* is going to pay good money for those leaves and has a right to every one of them, not half a leaf here and a third of a leaf there.

Speaking of leaves, you're not interested in the miserable one-leaf-per-stem look on a plant that you *know* is supposed to have leaves all up and down that stem. The shop has made some mistakes with this one. If you buy it and take it home, the shop's problem becomes your problem. More on the matter of leaves: An occasional yellow leaf on a plant is much like a few hairs in your comb. It's called normal attrition and is nothing to worry about. But—and this is a *big* but—lots of leaves yellowing and browning on a particular plant should make a loud gong go off in your head. Yes, feel sorry for the plant. But run the other way! If you want to see lots of leaves turning colors, be sure to take a pleasant junket to the country to view the autumn leaves. You *don't* want to see them on your houseplants!

On a lighter note—the matter of dust. While you have every right to expect better housekeeping, particulate matter on leaves is hardly a terminal condition. On the other hand, its presence does suggest that stock is not moving but has been sitting around literally collecting dust. But don't overreact and disqualify an otherwise perfectly healthy-looking specimen over a matter of a few specks. *Do* clean off those leaves when you get home, because dust clogs a plant's pores and interferes with its ability to "breathe."

Let's turn to a more serious subject—uninvited insect life. God forbid you should switch on the light one hot summer night and narrowly miss stepping on a big waterbug with your bare feet! You immediately draw the lines of battle and race for the Raid, right? Well, what we want you to do is to take that horror you reserve for waterbugs and channel some of it calmly and constructively when you shop for new plants. How do you do this? It's very easy. While you're considering a particular plant, pick it up and closely examine it in good light. In chapter 7 we'll talk at some length about specific bugs, exactly what they look like, which plants they tend to prefer, and how to get rid of them. For now, we're simply shopping and want to rule out plants that have the obvious presence of insect life.

Look over the plant in your hand carefully. Check the leaves. Pay particular attention to their undersides, because this site is a favorite resting, dining, and breeding place for many bugs. Also, be sure to check the newest growth. Just as you may prefer baby carrots to the full-grown variety, so do many insects prefer the tender growing tips of a plant to the older, hardened areas. Next, closely examine that little space above and below where a leaf joins a stem. These special little nooks are such popular hangouts for bugs that a plant could get rich just charging rent. If your examination thus far has not revealed any extra life forms other than the plant in the pot, chances are good that you have a bug-free specimen in your hand.

If, however, your inspection has turned up some six- or eight-legged creatures lurking in the recesses, *don't* drop the plant! After all, these aren't cockroaches! But by all means get that infested plant out of your hand and out of your mind. This one is not for you! By the way, let us assure you that there is no reason whatsoever to fear that the insects on a buggy plant are going to hop off that plant, march across the carpet, and jump into tonight's salad or make the leap onto you! Plants have insects specific to them and them alone.

Now a word about the good earth: While it should not prove terminal if a plant's soil is moderately inferior, the soil is always of interest to you, the prospective buyer. In chapter 4 we'll discuss what constitutes a good potting mixture. For now we simply want to identify a most serious, and fortunately *very* obvious, condition that you want to avoid.

Have you ever picked up a plant whose soil surface was as hard as a brick, the soil so firmly packed down you could literally bounce a ball off it? If this struck you as a little strange or perhaps downright amazing, your instincts were perfectly right. This soil is much too heavy. It lacks proper aeration for the roots. The helpless plant is literally cemented in place. And that's in its *dry* state. When it is wet, this strange mixture assumes the consistency of a mucky swamp. It practically drowns the plant. Either way, this soil is poor. One way or the other you are bound to suffer right along with the plant trapped in it. Yes, it's true that you can go ahead and buy the plant, take it home, and change the soil. But given the situation, this is not so easily accomplished as slipping out of one pair of shoes and into another. Freeing a plant from soil like this will cause further trauma to an already precarious root system. On the other hand, you can't leave it in that awful soil! So count to twenty when you contemplate taking on such a situation. The moral is: You can't just look at the plant. You have to look at what it comes in!

Speaking of soil and what lives in it, let's talk a moment about roots sticking out of drainage holes at the bottom of a pot. This sight is hardly a reason to run out of the shop with your hand clasped over your mouth. But this state of affairs tells you something important: The plant's root system is pot-bound; that is, roots have used up all the available space in the pot, and in search of somewhere to go, some have made their way out drainage holes. This event is much like having a party where so many guests show up that some have to stand in the doorway. It's no more a disaster for your plant than it is for your inconvenienced guests. In chapter 5 we'll talk about the why's and wherefore's of when and how to transplant a plant. For now, on our shopping tour, simply realize that caring for the plant with the maze of dangling roots is not easy. You can't bring this one home, take it out of the bag, plunk it down on the windowsill, and that's that. This one is going to need a new pot *right away!*

Let's switch to the other extreme—skimpy root systems. You may have already discovered that cacti and other succulents have surprisingly minimal roots relative to all that plant above the soil line. This is perfectly natural and normal. However, any other plant that flops and wobbles around in its pot *has* got a problem. It is laboring over an immature root system, one that was not allowed sufficient time to develop before it left the greenhouse where it was grown; it is still at a tender stage of development and requires tender treatment. Bringing home a plant like this is like buying a chick that needs further incubation, when you ordered and were prepared to take care of a chicken. *Let the plant shop take care of its chicks.* You're in the market for chickens.

Let's pause and take stock of your progress. We've identified where not to buy your plants. We've also identified those pitfalls that always handicapped your success with plants even before you left the shop. You're already feeling the difference that a little practical information can make. A new sharp glint in your eyes is overtaking that "green" (pardon the color) look you wore when you walked into that plant shop. You've become a wiser shopper, and your future plants will reward you for it!

2.

Once in the Right Place, How <u>Not</u> to Buy the Wrong Plants

Now that you finally know your way around the plant shop, garden center, and florist, it's time to pick out the right plants for you. So, you say, what *are* the right plants? Let us put it this way: No one can run up a list of the "right" plants for everyone. It's impossible. What is a perfect choice for you, with sun streaming through your huge windows, would be a perfect disaster for the guy living downstairs in the dark basement apartment. If you have all of ten minutes a week to lavish on your plants, you can't even consider duplicating the huge collection of fussy specimens the retired neighbor has happily growing in his home greenhouse. The trick is to match your plants with your specific conditions and abilities.

How do you do this? Before you consider humidity requirements, watering requirements, or any other kind of requirements, before you think about which plant would look good where, whether they grow up or down, sideways or backwards, the *first and most important issue is light*. That is, the amount of sun, or lack of it, that falls on the particular location in your home, apartment, office, or wherever else it is that you want to grow a plant.

As you're already well aware, there are dozens of plant books on the market today that tell you which plants must have Full Sun, which plants want Moderate Light (somewhere in between full sun and shade), and which plants tolerate Shade. For all practical purposes, these three categories cover all the bases for indoor plant cultivation. This book in no way seeks to duplicate the information that appears in the form of charts, lists, diagrams, and various depictions. All you have to do is open any reasonable plant book, flip over a few pages, and there it appears! What *this* book is telling you is to *believe* what you read!

To begin our discussion at the brighter side of the light spectrum, if a geranium is listed under the Full Sun category, don't think for a moment that anyone is kidding. Full Sun is full sun. If you, the possessor of low light, want to start a collection of African violets, turn to the chart for Shade. Are your precious violets listed here? No way! These are Moderate Light plants. But don't take the bad news personally. This business of matching plants with the available light is most impersonal! But ignore the rules, place the plant that is clearly listed as needing moderate light in the dark, and you'll get the message loud and clear when half its leaves fall off. Then you will suffer personally. What's more, your plant may become the victim of etiolation, or stretched growth, which occurs when a plant is placed in less sun than it needs and deserves. See photographs 1 and 2 to get an idea of how horrible stretched growth can look.

Are we making the point?

Please don't misunderstand: Many plants that prefer Full Sun (and are so listed) can be eased into the next lower light category of Moderate Light and still do quite well. We'll identify some of these plants as we go along. But in the meanwhile, do not delude yourself into thinking that there is any way you can talk the extreme of Sun into Shade.

"But wait a minute," you say, as many of our customers have said. "I bought a cactus a year ago, and they told me it wanted Full Sun. But we put it in the dining room where it's very dark, and the cactus is still living. It's still there! So what about this?" Well, let's talk about that. It does seem to be a blatant contradiction to the rule that says you can't tamper with extremes. Then what's the explanation for the sun-loving cactus relegated to the dark that appears to be okay? To explain, we'd like to tell you a story about a baby turtle. If you are like many of us, at some point in your childhood you were given a baby turtle as a pet. Probably neither you nor your parents, nor even the pet shop owner, had any understanding of the proper diet and all the rest that a baby turtle requires to stay alive. But where we all really fell short, where we missed the mark altogether, was in our ignorance of the fact that lots of sun is critical to the health and well-being of a hatchling turtle. But, ignorant of the facts, we put our turtle in that pathetic little plastic bowl with the runway that led up to the dry spot with the awful fake palm tree on top. Then we gleefully carried this bowl, housing our little pet, to a dim corner of our bedroom.

What happened to our turtle in the ensuing weeks and months? Did he grow? Did he thrive? Did he live long enough to become a big turtle? No, he did not. He never even made it out of the match-box size. What happened? Unlike mammals, who show signs of gross mistreatment promptly, reptiles take, if you will pardon the message, *a long time to die.* So, unbeknown to us, our little turtle began his slow but inevitable decline on the very first day he was denied the life-supporting sun. But, sadly, it took weeks and months for symptoms to show up. By that time, his shell was already soft. He became listless, and weeks after that he stopped eating. Later on, he stopped moving. Then one day he finally died. This old familiar story is the same story of today's cactus relegated to darkness.

How is it possible? First, your cactus in the dark is not growing. It subsists, and just barely. It's hanging on to life by threads that started to fray the first day you brought it home. Like the turtle, the die-hard cactus doesn't collapse overnight, look dead, and be dead the next morning. It takes a long time, a long time indeed. It starts with the inevitable rotting of roots, which means less and less water (and the nourishment dissolved in it) gets up to the body of the plant. Months later, what used to be a nice dark green cactus is now pale green. The deterioration caused by light deprivation can now be seen on the surface. Several weeks later, the cactus looks as though it's shriveling. A month later it is definitely shriveling. Another month later, things are really looking bad. The cactus is drying out like a huge cactus left out in the sun. One day you poke it with an exploratory finger to see if anything's alive in there, and lo and behold, you discover that what you have sitting in a pot in the dark dining room are the dried, stiff strands of a wizened shell of a plant that hasn't felt the surge of life in recent history. *It's dead.*

So the next time you're in the plant shop and you feel the urge for a cactus to "brighten up" that dark corner, what will you do? You'll remember the baby turtle and quietly move on.

But here's happy news! If you're one of the lucky ones blessed with full sun, go ahead and load up on cacti. Fill the room with them. They come in so many sizes and shapes and textures that you could stack them to the rafters and still have more species to explore. All are perfectly wonderful. Remember, we're not talking about the aforementioned miserable, depressed, stunted specimen struggling in the dark, ready to give up its pot for a ticket to the South for some decent sun! You've got the light, so go ahead and enjoy carefree luscious cacti full of vigor.

What other plants belong in the Full Sun and Moderate Light categories? What are more of the myths? Where are the trouble spots? Let's begin here: There is no flowering plant on earth cultivated as a houseplant that is going to produce a blossom in anything less than bright light! No matter what the label says! Now "bright" light does not necessarily mean full, blasting sun fourteen hours a day. The light can be moderately bright in some cases and still produce the desired results. But you can put money on the fact that *nothing* flowers in the dark. There are *no* exceptions.

What might appear to be an exception to this very strict dictum is the instance when you unknowingly purchase a flowering plant already in bud. You place it in dim light because that's all you have. Surprise! Those buds do open and blossoms unfold. You surmise from this lovely experience that indeed you can have flowers in your low light and that the bright light listing is wrong.

Well, it is our unhappy duty to inform you that the bright light listing was indeed right. What happened here was that the light necessary to trigger blooming occurred *before* you bought the plant. Despite its new dark corner, your plant is singing the flower song taught it in the sunny greenhouse or garden center where it was grown. But kept in the dark, this tune will be its solo performance, a cheery one-time aria. To give a repeat performance, that gifted plant must have the necessary bright light.

This doesn't mean you should wait for the last blossom to open and then toss out the whole business like a spent Kleenex. What it does mean is that you should be grateful for the show you happened to catch and then consider your options. You can resign yourself to a plant that will hereafter restrict itself to growing only leaves in your light. Or, in the spirit of seeing things live up to their full potential, you can give this plant to a deserving neighbor with a sunny window.

While we're on the subject of flowers and myths, let's shed some light on the flowering plant that has created more controversy in terms of care than practically any other—the African violet. Go to any bookstore or library and you'll see volumes and volumes dedicated to the cultivation of this plant. No doubt the sheer volume of all that advice suggests you need all that help, that here we have some kind of fragile beauty, some "shrinking" violet that no more can survive average care than a rose petal left out on a windowsill. Well, we're here to say *baloney!* Don't be intimidated by the high-strung hype or subscribe to the kid-glove treatment. If you treat this plant like a prima donna, it becomes a prima donna, and you'll unwittingly create a potful of oversensitized plant that will have you so frazzled you'll be afraid to breathe on it. So forget that nonsense and relax! If you can meet the bright light requirements of this star bloomer, the rest is a piece of cake. During the winter months, when the days are short and the sun's rays are at their weakest, place your violet in direct, unobstructed, Full Sun. During the summer months, when days are longer and the sun is overhead and more intense (and burning to an African violet), place your plant in very bright but *indirect* sun. This translates to Moderate Light. There you have it. That's all there is to it.

What other kinds of plants do we find listed in the bright light categories? Plants capable of variegation. What is "variegation"? Simply stated, it is colors other than green that occur in a leaf, stem, or any other part of a plant that has built into its genes this capacity for color. Photographs 3 and 4 show the difference between a plain green plant and a variegated plant.

What are some other examples of variegation in plants? In a corn plant *(Dracaena fragrans massangeana)* it is that broad streak of yellow that runs down each leaf. In its cousin, the *Dracaena marginata*, it is those red bands that edge the leaf. (See photograph 5.) In another variety, that spectacular *Dracaena marginata* 'Tricolor,' we see whites, pinks, all the way to splendid reds! (See photograph 6.) We see variegation in geraniums with leaves accentuated with wonderful white markings. We see it in 'Tricolor' jade plants, which sport white and pink in otherwise green leaves. We see it in several varieties of African violets, which delight the eye not only with their sometimes dual-colored flowers but also with cream-colored patterns in their leaves. Then there's the variegation that occurs in several varieties of rubber trees, whose leaves can be a combination of greens, white, cream, yellow, or solid burgundy. It even shows up in species of that last-ditch-when-all-else-fails snake plant that will throw out bands of beige and cream, and even white in some varieties.

What is the agent inside the plant that determines the capacity for color? It is the information contained in the genes. What is the agent outside the plant that activates the color switch already locked into the genes? What is the outside agent that is responsible for all this color, that provides such a feast for the eyes, that makes the world more beautiful? That agent is *light!* The point for us is: The *brighter* that light, the *more intense* the colors will be.

Let's turn to practical considerations and ask the following question: What happens when a variegated plant that has already displayed its full colors in bright light is purchased by you, the possessor of moderate to low light? The plant soon realizes it is in less sun. To the degree that the light is dimmer, the plant will reduce its variegation in the direction of plain green as new leaves are produced. So our equation reads: In a plant capable of variegation, the *less light* you have, the *more green* you'll see. We'll take this principle and apply it to a croton, a plant capable (depending upon the variety) of creating a veritable rainbow of colors in its leaves. Let's say you buy one loaded with color, which as you now know indicates it was grown in strong light. You take it home and place it in the moderate light spot where you want to grow it. What happens? The very next leaf that comes along in your lower light is already reverting to plain green. The next series of leaves will follow suit in an orderly fashion, producing more and more green. Let's say, for argument's sake, that six months later you move this plant to a really bright window. What will result? The process is reversed. The croton switches on the color and turns off the green. If you were inclined to strange experimentation, you could keep this up for years, creating a strange kind of "zebra." While it might get a little confusing for you, your plant will assume that it is in a land of remarkable climatic changes and continue to turn on and off the switch connected to its genes that controls variegation.

What other plants will always be listed under the bright light categories of Full Sun and Moderate Light? Well, let's not forget that small-leafed tree you see in so many homes, department stores, office buildings, hotel lobbies, and all over town, commonly referred to as a "fig" tree. Botanically it is termed a _Ficus_. Despite all this popularity, few trees have presented more people with more problems than the ubiquitous _Ficus_ tree! (Therefore, we have devoted a large section of chapter 10 to deal solely with this tree.) But the key word here is _preventable_. How so? Let us put it this way: If you want a gorgeous tree that will thrill you as it basks in glorious health, believe that chart and grow it in good light! If you want a dying tree full of lifeless twigs that is guaranteed to produce a discouraging pile of brown leaves on the floor, ignore that listing and put it in the dark. It's that simple.

Why struggle with a high light plant such as a _Ficus_ tree when, as any quick glance at a light chart will reveal, all sorts of Moderate Light plants, such as all of the palms and all the _Dracaenas_ and hanging plants (such as all of the ferns), are there for the choosing? Why try to buck the system and lose when you can so easily go with it and win?

As we leave that good light and go into Shade, we want to express one last thought: In several instances you'll find plants listed in not one but two light categories. What are you to make of this? Simply this: Any plant listed in two light categories will always prefer the *higher* one.

Let's use the spathe (*Spathiphyllum*) as an illustration. Place this plant in the tolerated but *not* preferred Shade, and your plant will restrict itself to green leaves only. Place this plant in the much preferred Moderate Light, and it will say a grateful thank you by producing a steady stream of extremely showy, long-lasting white flowers all spring and all summer. The shade-tolerant corn plant will do perfectly all right in the dim light, but give it some good Moderate Light, and it will send up a spike of delicate white flowers that grow more fragrant with each passing day. Even the snake plant flowers when put in bright light. So, if you have a choice, by all means opt for that brighter light.

What's left on the light charts? None other than our last category, the "forbidden" zone of Shade! Now, there is no reason whatsoever why shade should be perceived as some sentence of gloom and doom. Shade is shade. When all is said and done, if it's all you've got, *it's all you've got!* There's no point in comparing apples with oranges if you haven't got the light for apples! Eat the oranges. Enjoy the oranges. And be grateful you have them. To show you that you are hardly restricted to five measly plants, below is our own special listing of ten terrific plants for those of you who fumble around in the dark but still want some greenery to keep you company.

One: Let's start with the aforementioned corn plant (*Dracaena fragrans massangeana*). This is a wonderfully sturdy plant native to West Africa that grows (slowly) into a nice floor plant. It has broad and arching dark green leaves with a yellow band that runs down each leaf. If yours is really low, *low* light, as already mentioned, you're going to see less and less of that yellow band. But so what! Your plant can handle the loss, so make sure you can too!

Two: The *Dracaena* 'Janet Craig.' This plant's appearance is much like that of the corn plant, but with no variegation for you to watch fade into green. This plant is already all green. Like its cousin the corn plant, this one is developed from relatives native to Africa and is sturdy, sturdy.

Three: Back to some variegation. Try a striped Dracaena, the *Dracaena deremensis* 'Warneckii.' The remarkable news here is that even in very low light, this creature still somehow manages to keep that white streak going. How it does it, we don't know. Just be happy and enjoy it!

Four: The spathe plant (*Spathiphyllum*). There are a few varieties of these "peace lilies" from which to choose. One, the 'Mauna Loa,' is a very lovely plant that will stand some four feet tall at maturity. There are smaller varieties, such as the 'Clevelandii' and the dwarf *Spathiphyllum floribundum*. They all produce handsome, glossy-green leaves. (And yes, each is capable of producing those wonderful white flowers, but you'll never see them in your low light. So forget about them.)

Five: *Philodendrons!* And lots of species to choose from! Yes, it's certainly true that these climbing and hanging and standing plants wish they had some better light. So do you. But you don't have it. So feel free to load up on these shade-tolerant plants and be confident that they'll do just fine.

Six: *Scindapsus*, commonly referred to as pothos. There are several varieties of these hanging and climbing plants to choose from, all close cousins of the philodendrons. Many sport various cream and yellow markings in their leaves, which will fade in low light. But once again, the plant can handle it—it'll make the necessary adjustments—so relax and enjoy.

Seven: Grape ivy (*Cissus rhombifolia*). This is a lovely hanging vine with a most graceful, arching, trailing habit. Its cousin, kangaroo ivy (*Cissus antarctica*), has the same grace but a larger leaf. Both are remarkably sturdy, but in very low light they are easily ruined by too-frequent watering. (Be sure to see the following chapter about overwatering.)

Eight: Not the variegated but the plain green spider plant (*Chlorophytum*). Now don't be a snob and automatically emit: "Oh, I just hate spider plants!" This green variety is a perfectly beautiful plant when well grown. And there are no other low-light plants that will give you quite the full crown of green leaves that this one will! (By the way, for those of you interested in plant parenthood, spider plants send out those wonderful runners ending in baby plantlets.)

Nine: Aspidistra or cast-iron plant. This is the indestructible plant that our grandmothers had in the sunshaded sitting rooms of another century. Unfortunately, this plant is no longer readily available (because it grows so slowly), and it has also become extremely expensive. But if you can get your hands on one of these elusive specimens, grab it!

Ten: The Chinese evergreen (*Aglaonema*). This upright, handsome plant comes in several varieties, some of them plain green and some variegated. They're uniformly very sturdy. They grow slowly to attain heights of three feet or so at maturity.

So here are ten low-light, bona fide *true shade* plants to choose from. Lest we be called exclusionary, let's add a final one—that vastly maligned snake plant. This plant will take abuse, darkness, and even layers of city dust and grime, and still stand up to be counted! After this plant comes *plastic!*

So there you have it. Plants for Shade, plants for Moderate Light, and plants for Full Sun. Having dealt with the foremost consideration of light, we can now proceed to the other issues of choosing the right plants. We need to address the considerations of matching your plants with your specific abilities and free time; meeting the humidity requirements of some plants; and, last but not least, the big concern for households with small children or pets: the issue of poisonous plants.

What does it mean to match your plants with your abilities and free time? It means that if your natural inclinations do not include tending to detail and if you have precious little time for yourself, don't choose plants that need a lot of fuss to keep them happy. Let us use the African violet as an example of a plant whose care must include a regular pruning of spent flowers and old leaves. This pruning is not just to keep the plant well groomed and attractive but to keep it healthy. African violets are prone to fungus problems. Those faded blossoms and decomposing juicy leaves look mighty good to microscopic mold spores borne aloft in the air looking for somewhere to call home. So if you don't regularly look after your violets, it's only a matter of time before one fungus blight or another will look after them for you!

Let's look at another example—the aluminum plant (*Pilea*). This delightful plant comes in several shades of green with various metallic hues, and it couldn't be lovelier sitting on your moderately bright windowsill. It's easy to grow and relatively carefree except for one small detail: If you fail to pinch off its growing tips to induce branching all spring and summer, this sweet, pretty little plant turns into a leggy, stalky, disheveled mess.

Now we wouldn't want you to get the impression that African violets and aluminum plants are the only plants that need pruning. *All* plants at one point or another require snipping to keep them attractive, to keep them in bounds, and to keep them healthy. The point is, *some* plants require more than their share. If you love puttering around and giving a regular snip here and a pinch there, these "busy" plants are perfect for you. They'll give you, the indoor gardener, that "time well spent" feeling that suburban and rural gardeners enjoy after a regular good weed in the garden.

If you want a few general rules of thumb that separate the busy plant people from the laid back "let 'em (more of less) take care of themselves" folks, we offer the following generalizations: Small plants require far more care than large plants. How so? Since little pots dry out faster than big ones, small plants need watering far more often than large plants. Where small plants generally need transplanting to larger pots every year, large plants can skip a year, and sometimes two or three, between moves. Then there's the often painful question: "Who will take care of my plants while I'm away for two weeks?"

If yours is a sizable collection of small plants, you may make elaborate arrangements with the neighbor and leave three pages of notes: "Water the plain green one every day. Water the one with the fuzzy leaves every other day. Don't forget to check the one with flowers on the fourth day. I'll call you on the fifth day to see how you're doing." Contrast this exacting concern with the simplicity of the plant lover who has pared down his indoor greenery to three five-foot floor plants. This guy, whose nature does not include nurturing, gives the three green "big guys" a good drink before he leaves, sails out the door, and breezes into his vacation without a backward glance.

If you want to match your "no frills" self to the most "no frills" plants of all, look no further than cacti and succulents. With some two thousand species to choose from, you'll find enough plants to keep you happy for a lifetime. Compared to foliage plants, succulents grow very slowly, which means your transplants will be few and far between. No matter how small or large, their soil must be allowed to dry out between waterings, which means your watering can may collect dust in the intervals. While you're not spared fertilizing during the spring and summer months, when your succulents are actively growing, their need for pruning is minimal compared to regular leafy plants. If you appreciate the look, have the light, and identify with the stoic nature of these plants from the desert, you've found yourself a perfect match!

Let's now turn our attention to the next consideration for choosing the right plants for you—the issue of humidity. What is humidity? It is the moisture content in the air. What does it mean when it comes to your plants? It means that some plants need *high* humidity because they (or their ancestors) originated in tropical forests where the moisture content of the air is high, while some plants tolerate *low* humidity because they came from deserts or desertlike terrains where the moisture content is low. The remaining *moderate* humidity plants came from geographic areas neither moist nor dry but somewhere in between.

What does this tell you about caring for these different kinds of plants? It says you are going to have to provide high humidity for your tropical rain forest plants, don't worry about your arid desert dwellers, but do give some thought to the needs of your middle-of-the-road plants.

"How on earth am I supposed to know which plant comes from where?" you cry. Fear not. You don't need a plant encyclopedia, you don't need a labeled globe, and you don't need the help of fifty plant experts either. All you need is your own two eyes. Where do you direct them to look? At the shape and thickness of a plant's leaves. These two descriptives won't tell you a plant's country of origin, but they'll tell you something far more important—the *climate* of that region.

Let's look at the leaves of the common jade plant. The leaves are thick, fleshy, and succulent. What's in them to make them so plump? Stored water. Why does this plant store water in its leaves? Evolution has taught it that survival means more than the mere quenching of its thirst when the rains finally come. The stored water in its leaves will sustain it through droughts that stretch from weeks into months. What kind of geographic location has this sparse rainfall? A dry, desertlike terrain.

What kind of humidity occurs in a dry, desertlike terrain? *Low* humidity.

Let's look at the leaf, or frond, of a Boston fern. Is it plump? Is there a spare drop of water in there? Hardly! It's paper-thin. It contains just enough moisture to take care of its current needs. Is this a continuous and smooth-surfaced leaf like the jade plant leaf? Does it capitalize on minimizing the evaporation of water from the reduced surface area exposed to the air? No way! This fern frond is serrated all up and down and has crevices and indentations galore. Those indentations *increase* the surface area of the leaf exposed to the air, thereby promoting rapid moisture loss.

Do you think a leaf like this that gives off water vapor so freely would last one day in the hot dry air of a desert? It wouldn't last one hour. What is the only geographic locale that could provide the lush rainfall and moist air to prevent this lacy leaf from shriveling? A tropical forest. What kind of humidity occurs in a tropical forest? *High* humidity.

What does a leaf that is somewhere between succulent and paper-thin tell you? It says the plant originated in a terrain that is neither arid nor moist but somewhere in between. What can we say about the humidity that occurs in such a locale? That it is neither high nor low but *moderate*.

Now that you know how to tell with one glance the humidity needs of a plant, you're that much closer to knowing which plants are right for you and which are wrong. If squeezing the trigger on the mister bottle fifteen times a day makes you feel like Mother Nature bathing her rain forest plants in humidity, your indoor paradise should include lots of thin-leafed plants, such as ferns. If five sprays with the mister has you ready to call it quits, choose plants, such as *Peperomias*, *Pileas*, Wandering Jews, and spathe plants, with moderate humidity needs. If you hate misting, go for one of the two thousand species of cactus and succulent that don't want that high humidity any more than you're interested in providing it.

Last, we come to the issue of poisonous plants. If your household includes small children or chewing pets, such as dogs, cats, birds, and hamsters, you will want to know some of the plants that pose a threat to these family members. Needless to say, you'll eliminate them from consideration on your plant-buying trips, and if you discover you already have an offender in your midst, you'll relocate it to a spot well beyond the reach of little fingers and indiscriminate mouths. Or better yet, give the plant away.

Which houseplants are poisonous? We're sorry to say that the list starts with the plant family *Araceae*, which includes the sturdy, shade-tolerant philodendrons and that popular floor plant the dumbcane (or *Dieffenbachia*). Which parts of these plants are toxic when ingested? *All* parts. While hardly as popular, and in a different plant family altogether, all parts of the flowering oleander are also poisonous.

Long before the first crocus rears its head in the outdoor garden, the profusion of colorful caladiums and flowering azaleas and fragrant hyacinths in the marketplace tells the winter-weary that spring is around the corner. Unfortunately, these preseason offerings also herald the sudden rise of accidental poisonings in the home. How so? All parts of the showy caladium are poisonous. The leaves and colorful flowers (but not the stems) of azaleas are also poisonous. While the heady fragrance of the hyacinth flower is such a welcome breath of spring, the bulb beneath that plant is toxic.

The cool crisp air of fall brings yet another trouble plant: the Jerusalem cherry *(Solanum)*. The little red fruits this plant produces are fascinating to a curious two-year-old. But beware, they're poisonous!

If spring and fall host some bad news for households with the patter of little feet, the holidays in December are fraught with danger. That little sprig of mistletoe coyly hanging from the ceiling does more than promote holiday cheer and romantic merriment. From it fall little berries that are poisonous when ingested.

The most prevalent toxic offender of all is the poinsettia. With its red bracts (not flowers at all but modified leaves), this plant has come to symbolize Christmas. Its real name is *Euphorbia pulcherrima*. The problem is that, as with other *Euphorbias* (crown of thorns, *Euphorbia splendens*, candelabra cactus, *Euphorbia lactae*), when any part of the poinsettia is punctured, torn, or eaten, it exudes a white sap that can be extremely irritating to the tissues of people and pets. So, by all means let the holidays find you and yours in good spirits, but save this plant for when the kids are grown!

P.S. Do you sneak new plants into your home and then wait with bated breath to see if they'll be the next victims of the marauding claws and teeth of your otherwise hospitable cat? Are you tired of having your present plants torn to shreds? Are you sick of playing the old cat-and-plant game? Then put an end to this desecration, and let one sentence point the way: Most cats prey on plants with thin, long leaves. Which plants are these? They're plants such as palms, spider plants, and

Dracaena marginatas. What can you do about it? Put these plants out of your cat's reach and don't bring home any more that will appeal to your cat!

Before you read this chapter, your plant purchases were motivated by fiction, not fact. By fantasy, not reality. By impulse, not deliberation. By whim, not wisdom. With all that scientific method going for you, is it any wonder that nine out of ten of these ill-conceived, ill-advised plant purchases proved disastrous? What do you know now that you never knew before? You know how to match your home environment and abilities with the appropriate plants. Finally you know, once you get to the right place, how *not* to buy the wrong plant!

3.

How Not to Ever Overwater Your Plants Again

Before you read another word, I want you to take a good hard look at photograph 8.

What on earth is the matter with this plant? Why does it look so awful? Why all the yellow leaves? Why all the brown tips? Why does it look so limp? Why has it lost half its leaves?

We'll make it very simple: This is a picture of an over-watered plant. This is a plant that is midway between life and death via the simple instrument of the watering can!

Is this a rare occurrence? Is this affliction, this addiction to the watering can a sometime occurrence with you, the public? After bad choices in plants, over-watering is the absolute number-one cause of death in houseplants. It happens so often that we have no doubt one could build a highway from New York to Los Angeles with all the soggy carcasses of the world's over-watered plants and still be able to go on to Hawaii. That's how common it is.

But take heart, all you overwaterers out there! You

are about to be cured. Read this chapter, and we guarantee you'll never overwater a plant again.

How can we promise this? Here's how: We are going to teach you a revolutionary new approach to watering that answers the two nagging questions you have asked in frustration a hundred times as you watched your plants yellow and die. The first is, "How *often* do I water?" The second is, "How *much* do I water?"

In order for you to appreciate the simplicity and merits of this new system, you first have to have some understanding of what happens to a plant when it is overwatered. You're familiar with what happens on the outside: Leaves turn yellow at the bottom of a plant and continue to do so right on up the stem. Yellow discoloration at the tip and center of leaves eventually swallows up the entire leaf. Stems become weak and spindly. Finally, a wilt in the dilapidated foliage spells nothing less than disaster.

But what happens to the *inside* of the plant? What's going on there? To understand this requires a brief appreciation of how leaves are affected by the condition of the roots that supply them with water and nourishment. Reduced to the basics, it works like this: Every plant maintains a proportion of so many roots to so many leaves. In a healthy plant that is not doused every five minutes, this proportion of roots to leaves is self-sustained in a beautiful synchronization. When the soil dries out, a plant feels thirsty. It needs water to sustain itself. Along you come, the caretaker, to administer some relief. You pour water onto the surface of the soil. It filters down to the roots, which absorb and direct it to the openings of the plumbing system contained in the stem. The water is pulled up and evenly distributed throughout the leaves. The plant is now satisfied, and all is well.

This remarkably effective and simple system has worked since plants made their appearance on earth some three billion years ago. But let's see how this perfect system is perversely disrupted when a plant is over-watered, which means *watered too soon*. Here sits our case study plant with saturated soil. It will not need watering for another good month, but along you come, watering can in hand, and by some mysterious process you divine that it's time to water. Water seeps downward through the soil. In a moment it reaches the same roots that already have more than adequate moisture surrounding them. What do the roots do with this new water? Equally relevant, what happens to the roots themselves?

First things first: The roots do what Nature programmed them to do. They pull up the water and send it to the veins in the stem. The veins pull it up and send it to the network of leaves that were thought to be thirsty. But the leaves aren't thirsty! They already have plenty of water in them. And now they have a special delivery of water that they never ordered, don't need, and don't want.

What happens now? Well, the leaves must somehow accommodate all this water. But, as you are no doubt beginning to see, the cells that make up the leaf are already full, so the normally rigid cell walls stretch themselves to take in the extra water. What we now have are cells pushed to the breaking point. If the overwatering stopped here, we might just have a plant filled to the gills with water, with the dams still holding. But look. Two days have passed. Lurking in the corner is the watering can. Sitting on the sofa is you. You glance at the plant. It looks "funny." The leaves look limp somehow. (Waterlogged is more like it!) "Why doesn't it look crisp?" you ask yourself. "It must need water. That's it! I didn't water it enough!" So you get up, grab the can, and pour in a little more because that's the only thing you know to do.

We have now reached the breaking point. Water eventually reaches the cell walls that are literally ready to burst. And they do. The cell walls rupture, and water slides into the neighboring cells on all sides. They can't handle the extra water any better than the first ones, so their walls give way too. On it goes like a row of dominoes, as cell after cell falls.

Three days later you walk by the plant. There are several leaves with these funny soft yellow spots on them. "What on earth are these?" you ask. "They look terrible!" The next day you check the plant right away. There are many more leaves with soft yellow areas, and the tips of almost all the leaves are yellow and translucent. Some of them are brown. And good heavens, there are several leaves that are completely yellow. See photograph 7. What's happening here? What's going on? "I know I watered it. I watered it the other day!" you tell yourself. Then you remember your friend next door who says yellow leaves are caused by underwatering. "That's got to be it!" you tell yourself. So what do you do? You reach for the watering can.

With this scenario in mind, let's zoom back inside the plant and take a look at the other half of this story—the roots. With the first unnecessary dousing of the soil, the roots did two things. First, they did their job. They absorbed the water. But they also did something else as they continued to be doused over and over again: They started to rot, and die.

If we can go back and recall our basic principle that says every plant maintains a direct proportion of so many roots to so many leaves, it is not too hard to figure out what happens to our plant now. If X amount of roots are damaged or die from too frequent waterings, that same percentage of damage or death occurs to the leaves maintained by them.

In slight damage to roots, you see brown- and yellow-tipped leaves and occasional yellow areas in the center of leaves. In more than moderate damage, you have several yellow leaves. In extreme overwatering where one-third of a plant's root system is rotted out, so also will one-third of that plant's leaves yellow, then brown out. If 100 percent of the root system is destroyed, 100 percent of that plant's leaves yellow, turn brown, die, and fall off. Your plant is now dead. (See photograph 9.)

This marching progression of yellow leaves heralding a brown death is pretty much the scenario of the majority of houseplants that succumb to the watering can. But there are some plants that are so sensitive to excessive watering that they skip a few stages and get right down to the grim business of a fast death. As sturdy and easy to grow as they are, *Peperomias* are a perfect case in point. These plants are not as polite as their green comrades who drop little hints in the form of a brown-tipped leaf here and a yellow leaf there. Hardly! With *Peperomias*, two ill-timed strikes with the watering can and you're out! Deluge these plants one time too many at midnight, and by seven the next morning you'll find your plant promptly rotted out at the base line, where the stem emerges from the soil. You'll find your plant keeled over, lying on top of the soil like a lump of limp, overcooked spinach.

We assure you that many of the succulents also have an interesting way of saying that they have had it with the watering can. Like the *Peperomias*, you may wake one fine morning to find one dead root system in a soggy pot and the rest of the mushy plant on the floor. But few sights can rival what a cactus turns into when grossly overwatered. Take the case of a circular barrel cactus. Do you remember horror films in which the hero touches a face and the skin gives way, dissolving into mush and soft guts? Well, what a barrel cactus does with too much water is state-of-the-art fright. So you see, some plants will tolerate the old swamp treatment for about five minutes before they revolt.

Before we answer the age-old questions—"How often do I water?" "How much do I water?"—first a few emphatic words. Dismiss from your head once and for all the notion, the myth, the *absolute untruth* that a plant is to be watered once a week! How it came about, we don't know. But somewhere along the line this "watering by the week" myth entered and got stuck in the minds of 90 percent of our populace, despite the fact that it doesn't work. *It never worked!* Recently at The Village Green we spent as much as half an hour with a resistant customer carefully detailing our simple answer to the critical watering question, only to have the customer come back with, "Yes, I understand. . . . But how many times a week do I water?" We therefore strongly suggest that you obliterate from your mind any system of watering that has the word "week" in its vocabulary.

Let us explain why. Plants are living, breathing, growing creations. Just as you and I do, they have seasons of growth and change, and seasons of rest. Every cell, every pore of their being is affected by the presence and quality and duration of light, relative humidity, air temperature, air circulation, whether they have adequate space for growth, and the nature of the pot in which they are contained. Plants are also affected by the fertilizer they ingest in much the same way you and I are what we eat. So you can see how perfectly ridiculous it is to ignore all the variables that affect a plant and treat it as though it were a piece of lead piping sticking out of a pot that has to be oiled every two weeks according to the Owner's Manual. A plant is to be watered *when and as it needs it!*

Now let us answer the "How often do I water?" question so that you'll never overwater a plant again. Remember the discussion of how leaves work with roots? Choose a plant from your collection on the windowsill right now to see if you have a candidate ready for watering. Is there one whose soil surface looks dry? Touch it with your finger. Does it feel dry? If the answer is yes, go ahead and poke your finger further down into the soil. Is this soil dry too? If the answer is also yes, chances are this plant is ready for watering. But how do you know for sure? How can you see what's going on in the soil beyond what your finger can reach? Unless you have X-ray vision, the answer is you can't know for sure. Therefore, *do nothing.* Wait until the plant does something that tells you what is going on inside its pot. What on earth can a plant do to tell you that it needs water? It will do what every foliage plant is guaranteed to do as it begins to experience a water deficit at its roots—*it will wilt!*

Now we're not talking about the drastic, life-threatening, keeled-over-the-pot wilt that a plant exhibits when days and days have elapsed beyond the first day that the plant should have been watered. Not at all! We're talking about that first ever-so-slight downward tilt of the leaves that tells us the plant is right at the point and in fact is crossing over the point when it needs some water.

Something very important is happening at this moment. For the first time in your life, you know for certain there is no way that you are about to overwater this plant which, as you now know, means watering it too soon. Your plant is showing you beyond a shadow of a doubt that it needs water. There's no guesswork, no divining rods, no worry, no insecurity about doing the wrong thing, no if's, and's, or but's. There's just hard empirical evidence. As the plant starts to wilt, water it!

What happens after the watering? The slight wilt corrects itself. The leaves go right back to their original position. The plant should now be left alone until it next demonstrates to you its need for water. It's that simple. (See photograph 10.)

This "wait for a wilt" system covers regular foliage plants such as *Peperomias*, philodendrons, ferns, and all those plants with regular leaves that *can* wilt. But what about succulents? What happens, for instance, to the thick fleshy leaves of a jade plant that has run out of water or to a cactus that has only spines for leaves? If you're thinking that the leaves of a jade plant don't exactly wilt, you're right. These leaves do the same thing the body of a cactus does when it is overdue for a rain: They shrivel. The slight shriveling of a succulent is equivalent to the slight wilt in the leaves of a regular foliage plant. With a good watering, the affected leaves or stems plump out again to resume their former shape and texture.

At this point we joyfully add that this "wait for a symptom" system of watering also addresses a whole host of your other nitty-gritty watering questions. Which plant dries out faster, the one in the clay or in the plastic pot? The hanging plant or the upright? The plant in the bright window or its twin across the room on the coffee table? The moist bathroom plant or the tortured kitchen plant? The little six-inch plant or the six-foot floor monster? Plants with small root systems or plants with big root systems? The plant on the cool porch or the plant in the warm sitting room? These and any similar questions you could possibly come up with are answered with a quick and easy, "It doesn't matter!" It doesn't matter who, what, where, or which plant because one way or another the laws of Nature dictate that—be it overnight or in two months—every plant must eventually run out of water, and it will give you a sign. It will either wilt or shrivel, at which point—*and at no other*—you water.

You may already be asking whether it hurts a plant to let it wilt or shrivel ever-so-slightly. The answer is an emphatic but qualified no! This system openly and loudly directs you to go for a superficial risk in order to avoid and cancel out the profound risk of a losing battle with the number-one killer of houseplants. It's like going for a single harmless sneeze in order to sidestep a case of pneumonia with terminal overtones. A plant will always recover from a wilt or shriveling after you give it a thorough watering. Nature has designed plants to withstand a drought a hundred times more severe than the slight thirst we are recommending. But this is not the case with the overwatered plant. Here the ground floor, the very foundation has been seriously undermined. Roots have rotted and died. The plant is seriously debilitated. Now it is not just a sitting duck but a sick sitting duck— waiting for the inevitable onslaught of secondary complications such as fungus and insect infestations. And we won't remind you what *that* looks like.

Now that you know, with absolute confidence, how often to water a plant, let's find out how *much* to water. This issue is even simpler, if you can believe it, than the "how often." It is summed up in the following six words: *When it rains, it should pour.* What does this mean? It means drench instead of drizzle, soak instead of trickle. It means stop tiptoeing through your collection of houseplants with a dainty teacup doling out a teaspoon of water here and there. When you water a plant, soak it. Whether your plant is in a clay or plastic pot, hanging or standing, big or little, growing upwards, downwards, or sideways, flowering or foliage, in blasting sun or in dark recesses—when it's time to water it, you must pour in enough to saturate every particle of soil in that pot. That's how much water.

How do you achieve this kind of watering? Any number of ways. A few small portable plants can easily be brought to the sink, where room-temperature water is allowed to softly and thoroughly seep into every crevice of soil. After this, wait ten minutes or so. Then, because dry soil tends to reject water initially, pretend you never watered at all and soak the soil again. Give your plant another fifteen minutes to absorb any additional water from the soil that it may need. Let the pot drain. Your plant has now been thoroughly watered, and you can return it to its permanent site.

What about a hanging plant that comes in the ubiquitous plastic pot with the little saucer attached? Well, don't be fooled by that little saucer! It may look like it's doing something, but the amount of water it holds wouldn't qualify it for a finger bowl. Expecting that saucerful of water to help a thirsty plant is tantamount to giving a parched marathon runner at the twenty-eighth mile a Dixie cup of water! Therefore, let's move on to two thorough-soak techniques for hanging plants.

The first directs you to take down your hanging basket and give it the watering-in-the-sink treatment. Once again, as with any plant, one soaking isn't enough, so water twice. Water three times if you like. Each time, be sure to give the plant enough time to quench its thirst. Water the plant doesn't need will simply overflow into the sink.

You may say, "I hate carrying plants around. It's hard enough trying to keep track of the cat! I want my plants to stay put." But if you're like most people, watering an overhead basket is a tricky and frustrating business because you're always worried (and rightly so) about waterfalls cascading either down your arm (a sobering experience, to say the least) or headed for the floor and carpet. Your waterings therefore tend to be a fast flash with the can. The net result for your plant is a two-second douse that leaves major portions of a thirsty root ball dry as a bone. In time, the unhappiness of those dry roots will be reflected in the deteriorating condition of the leaves.

This is no way to water a plant you care about. To replace the fast hit-and-miss technique we suggest the slow-down-and-repeat method. When it's time to water, *slowly* pour a little water into the pot. Wait a few minutes so that the water is absorbed. Then add a little more water and let it seep down too. So far we've avoided a flood! Now go off to do something else for a while (maybe start the same procedure for a neighboring plant that's also due for a rain). Fifteen minutes later, go back to the plant and give it yet another drink. The idea is to repeat the water-and-wait technique as many times as necessary to soak all the soil in a particular pot, without torture to your arms or floors. As you can see, this method can't duplicate the perfect carefree soak the plant would get at the sink, but it's ten times better than your old way of watering.

For the remainder of your houseplants we introduce an invaluable, inexpensive, simple piece of equipment—the waterproof saucer. The waterproof saucer makes possible carefree, thorough watering of plants. As attractive as they are, standard clay saucers are *not* waterproof. Nor are the so-called new and improved water-resistant clay saucers. Both are porous. Eventually, if not immediately, both will permit moisture to seep down onto whatever they are sitting on. Waterproof means *plastic*. Plastic saucers, while available in many colors, are most often white and green. They also come in clear transparent varieties that go with anything. For those purists among you wed to the classic terra-cotta look, clay-colored plastic saucers are the newest thing.

What are you supposed to do with all these wonderful plastic saucers, clay-colored or otherwise? The idea is to put one under every single standing pot in your collection. What for? Let's recall the last time you watered your five-foot floor plant. You weren't sure whether it needed it because you never read this chapter before.

Nonetheless, you grabbed the watering can and poured some water onto the soil. Lo and behold, what happened? If your watering was akin to most people's experience with large plants, the water barely moistened the surface of the soil before it raced down that free-fall space so often created between a big root ball and the pot, and then gushed out onto the floor! You threw the watering can down and rushed for the paper towels to mop up the mess. The experience jangled your nerves, but you knew you had to get a grip on yourself and try adding a little more water because, after all, this is a big plant. So you poured some more water in. This time you were prepared. You had reams of paper towels ready to shove into the drainage holes to catch the deluge. Race out it did, right back onto that same patch of floorboards you just mopped up. "That's it!" you shouted. "I've had it! I can't stand the mess." You marched away frustrated, the floor took a beating again, and your five-foot plant had a watering that wouldn't satisfy a little six-inch plant.

Let's take this same plant with a saucer under it. Having read this chapter, you wait for the slight wilt in your plant's foliage that tells you it's time. With total confidence you reach for the watering can and slowly you begin to pour room-temperature water onto the surface of the soil. As before, the water barely wets the hard, dried surface before it runs out the drainage holes. But this time there's no need for paper towels and mops because our saucer is doing exactly what we want it to do—it is collecting water.

Like smaller plants, large plants must be allowed sufficient time to pull up the needed water. Since we're now dealing with a five-footer with a lot of foliage in need of a water delivery, this time we're not talking minutes but hours—maybe several of them. To be exact, the plant needs as many hours as it takes to recover from the visible evidence of its thirst. If you check the saucer after, say, one hour, and it is empty, check the plant. Does it still show some wilt? Then pour in more water. If after a few hours the wilt has completely corrected itself and the saucer is empty, you can walk away from this plant absolutely confident that its total water requirement has been met. You watered on time, you watered enough, and your nerves are still intact.

For your further edification, let's say that the final saucer check, after the wilt corrects itself, reveals some water still sitting in the saucer. What does this tell you? It says that the needs of this plant have already been served and that the water in the saucer is unnecessary. In order to prevent any damage to roots sitting in water that they don't want and can't absorb, empty the saucer. You can let a kitchen sponge do the job. With lightweight plants, simply lift the saucer out from under the pot and throw the water out.

Thus, the answer to the "how much water" question that has spoiled your greenery and haunted your dreams is simple: *as much as the plant needs!* The same procedure applies to small plants and medium-sized plants, whether they're housed in clay or plastic and whether they flower or just produce foliage. *No matter what they do, the rules are the same.* The beauty of this technique is its sheer, utter simplicity.

Speaking of things that work and do exactly what they're supposed to do, here's a very positive word about moisture meters. They're the little gadgets available in most plant shops that retail for under ten dollars. There are few other devices in the horticultural world that we can endorse with as much enthusiasm as this one. This gadget requires no batteries and lasts indefinitely. It reads the moisture content in the soil of a pot. On its head is a gauge that runs from one to ten, one being bone-dry and ten the saturation point. When the reading falls within one and three, it is equivalent to our system's slight-wilt or shriveling. At that point—and not before—use one of the thorough-soak methods. Don't leave the meter stuck in the soil all the time. Simply employ it when you suspect that a plant might be due for a soaking. The meter will either confirm or deny your suspicion.

An important footnote to the above: As wonderful as this tool is, it is accompanied by a little pamphlet outlining the manufacturer's ideas about various houseplants and their watering needs. Permit us to inform you that not only is this pamphlet *not* helpful, but the information contained therein is completely incorrect and misleading. Throw it away!

Before we leave this chapter we want you to know that we have not forgotten those of you who are trying to deal with one, two, or maybe dozens of soggy, overwatered plants. You might be wondering if there is anything you can do *now* to reverse their condition. Or is the prognosis all bleak? Well, frankly, the survival rate depends upon the extent of the damage, but no matter what the plant's condition, the procedure for recovery is more or less the same.

The first thing you want to do is *stop all watering*. If need be, put the watering can on the top shelf of the closet to get it out of reach. The second thing, as our chapter on fertilizing will detail, is eliminate fertilizing of any kind. An overwatered plant is in a state of distress. To ask it, by way of applying fertilizer, to grow at this point is like asking a patient who has just been wheeled back from surgery to get up and run. We're not interested in spectacular feats such as growth from a sick plant; for now, all we're asking the plant to do is survive. An imprudent dose of fertilizer to our green friend in intensive care just might push it over the hill. So no lethal "vitamins," please!

Next, we recall that our yellowing patient dropping leaves by the minute is sitting over a damaged, reduced root system. If this plant is indeed suffering from advanced overwatering, you'll notice a definite wilt in the remaining leaves. This wilt is not one that indicates the plant needs water! The leaves are wilting because so many roots have rotted out that now there aren't enough roots to get enough water to the leaves still hanging in there. This root-rot-induced wilt is a tricky touch-and-go situation. If you do nothing, chances are the plant will die. Therefore, you do the only thing that will give this plant a shot at survival: You prune! Pruning back the foliage reduces the burden on the struggling root system. The idea is that with a little luck the root system just might recover fast enough to muster the strength to take care of the leaves still remaining on the plant and start pushing out some new roots.

How much of the foliage do you prune off? If the wilt is moderate, assume that one-third of the roots are no longer functioning and prune back, in proportion, one-third of the plant's foliage. If the wilt looks bad, cut back half the plant. If it looks absolutely awful (which means

Pruning off one-third of its foliage to stabilize plant, which lost one-third of its roots to rot very few roots are in working order), you may have to prune considerably more, perhaps to within inches of the soil line. If you need help pruning, refer to chapter 8.

If you're lucky, your plant just might make it. Its rebirth will be heralded by the appearance of new stems and leaves. If you're unlucky, things may have already progressed to the point of no return.

Is there anything else you can do to help revive an overwatered plant? Yes, there is. Pray!

4.

How <u>Not</u> to Have a Potting Mixture That Dries Out Like a Brick and Wets Down Like a Swamp

Would you agree that a good brownie mix is essential to good brownies? Would you also agree that there's no point in building a wonderful castle on a sinking foundation of sand? Are we in accord that, no matter how terrific you look, if your feet hurt you're gonna feel lousy?

Good! Then you should have no problem understanding the fundamental fact that a poor potting mixture handicaps your plant right from the start. A poor potting mixture locks the roots (those critically important conduits for water and nourishment upon which the entire plant depends) into a foundation of mediocrity. And what do mediocre foundations produce? Bland brownies, castles that topple, low spirits that teeter over tight shoes, and plants that at best will always be fundamentally disadvantaged and at worst will grapple with death every day. Why on earth (pardon the pun) pot a perfectly nice plant in a bad potting mixture when as easy as one-two-three you can put together a batch of the good earth that will launch your plant into a real fighting chance at the good life!

Twelve years of experience at The Village Green has taught us that if things get too complicated, the instructions too detailed, at some point the customer stops listening. It isn't that you don't care to learn. You care very much about your plants and what affects them. The problem is, with everything that's going on in your life, your job, the roof that's leaking, the kids who are coughing, the cat who's overdue for her shots, you just don't have the time (or the energy) for long, complicated discourses on the merits of one soil mixture and the detractions of another. You've got to get your soil information straight and fast.

Good! No problem. Here are the bare facts of the Potting Soil Saga. First, the bad news. There is not one commercially prepared soil mixture on the market today that should be used right as it comes out of the bag. Now we know this is not what you wanted to hear, particularly since it's so convenient to pick up a bag or two at your local garden shop or supermarket. But facts are facts. Furthermore, we don't think we're bursting any bubbles. If you've used them, you already know these "quick fix," prepackaged soils that claim to be the very essence of the good earth *do not work*. Why don't they work? Across the board and without exception these commercial mixes have a fatal flaw that pivots on the word "water." In other words, "brand" potting soil is so constituted that when it dries out, what you have in the pot is a hard brick that cements the roots in place. This brick rejects water just like rain is repelled off a duck's back. But it isn't funny or cute, and it certainly isn't useful! Thirsty roots that can't get any water cannot send that same water up the stem to parched leaves. Leaves that don't receive water have a funny way of not living too long.

What's the flip side of the arid desert? The monsoons! When the typical Brand X mix finally wets down (a monumental feat in itself that requires the pot to spend the weekend submerged in the tub), it turns into a swamp. By the time the muck finally does dry out, the generous splashes of yellow leaves all over an otherwise green plant tell you that somewhere along the line (day four? day twenty?) large portions of your root system rotted out. So, wet or dry, either way you lose!

"What's the problem here?" you're asking, no doubt recalling with a sinking heart the generous stash of Miracle Earth under the sink. You're now starting to believe what your eyes told you years ago—that Miracle Earth hardly delivered the guaranteed miracles. You're also wondering if it is so hard to put together a little bag of soil that works. Can an entire industry be wrong? Is a decent potting mixture something only a scientist with fifteen letters after his name can concoct in a laboratory? Let's take these questions in order. No, it isn't at all hard to put together a good potting soil. Yes, an entire industry is wrong. And no, you don't have to be a scientist to get it right.

The fact is few things are as simple in the horticultural world as putting together a nice little batch of the good earth. Before we get to that, let's see if we can reconstruct the source of the anxiety and insecurity that drove you out into the world of prepackaged wonders in the first place. If we are not mistaken, it went something like this: Way back in the beginning when you brought your first houseplants home, you thought you'd like to know something about them, so you went to the bookstore and picked up a few books about plants. It was wonderful! It was fun poring over all the pictures, finding out which of your plants was native to where, how they grew, and what to expect. But then one day you needed to transplant a few plants. This is where the fun reading stopped and the anxiety began.

How did it happen? Let's recall. There you were at the kitchen table eyeing your African violet, a couple of philodendrons, a *Dracaena*, two succulents, and a cactus. All you wanted was a simple little recipe for a proper potting soil. The day was Friday, and you'd carefully designated Saturday as "transplant day." You were already aware that you couldn't just run out in the backyard and scoop up some dirt with a spoon. You knew that houseplants require a good, fresh, sterilized soil in which to grow, but you'd forgotten exactly what constituted a good mixture. So you turned to what was supposed to be the source of useful and reassuring information—the chapter on soil in one of your books. Suddenly and without warning, instead of the simple little formula you wanted, you were faced with no less than eighteen soil mixes to choose from. There was one for the violet, three for the *Dracaena*, four for the philodendrons, and yet another for the succulents. And heavens no!—there was one last one to cover the cactus! "This is impossible!" you cried, the idea of fun flying right out the window. "I have a few hours tomorrow to do this, not a month! I need *one* soil mixture that will take care of everybody!"

So you read on. Four exasperating pages later, as your hair was starting to curl, it looked as though you'd found it! The heading read: A Good All-Purpose Potting Mixture. Terrific! At last—deliverance from confusion and toil! But look at this! The recipe that promised utter simplicity had you gather together *only* the following:

6 cups of soil
2½ cups of perlite
2¾ cups of vermiculite
5⅝ cups of peat moss
2½ cups of sand
2½ tablespoons of granular fertilizer
¾ tablespoon of charcoal
⅝ cup of leaf mold
A "dash" of well-rotted cow manure

"What is all this?" you wondered. "What on earth are all these ingredients?" And look at that, a "dash of well-rotted cow manure." As we all know, you always make a point of keeping that around the house!

This was the "simple formula"—the "easy to mix," everyday recipe for the average houseplant that you were supposed to effortlessly throw together in between pruning your African violet. It is no wonder that, as you looked around and imagined every vessel in your house labeled and soiled with all these wondrous ingredients, you threw up your hands and yelled, "This is impossible!" Even if you could gather together all this stuff, you'd have to move to a larger house, host a Tupperware party to stock up on all the containers, get rid of your husband, throw the kids out, quit your job, and devote what was left of your life to this "simple" task of having various strange ingredients on hand and ready to mix every time you wanted to pot a philodendron.

In fear and exasperation, you shoved the cat out of the way, threw on your coat, and headed straight for the supermarket in search of relief. With the same spirit of defeat and intimidation that has you reach for a frozen cake instead of putting a ridiculously complicated recipe together at home, you grabbed your first bag of Miracle Mix.

Relief *is* on the way! And we don't mean the phony fix in the printed plastic bag that is overpriced. We mean real relief in the form of an honest-to-goodness perfect soil mix that, if you can count from one to three, is yours for the making. So, to get down to basics that really work, here is *The Village Green's Simple Formula for a Great Potting Mixture*. This is the mix for people whose lives cannot and do not pivot around transplanting their plants. Unless we're talking about the most foreign and exotic of orchids, the most *epiphytic* of the epiphytic brome-liads, or the mushroom culture in the cellar, we promise that this one will nicely cover all your general potting needs. But remember: If you want to get fancy and mix up something more specialized, you know what to do. Go to your other plant books that give you eighteen recipes and choose one!

Three ingredients make up this mix. The first is soil, as in dirt. The only qualification is that you use sterilized dirt. At your garden center or in the supermarket, pick up a bag of sterilized topsoil. Still with us? Ingredient number two is peat moss. All you have to do is ask the same person who gave you the topsoil for a bag of peat moss, or pick it up at the supermarket too. It's nothing bizarre or exotic, it's just plain old peat moss. The label will say so. For our third ingredient we want something for drainage in our soil. That something can be a sub-stance called perlite, vermiculite, or sand. Some people prefer perlite over vermiculite, and vice versa. Others swear by sand. Still others like to use a combination of all three substances. Personally, we prefer perlite, but the point is that any one or any combination of these will do. So here we are, one-two-three:

Ingredient #1: Soil
Ingredient #2: Peat moss
Ingredient #3: Sand or perlite or vermiculite
(or any combination)

That's it! This is our basic all-purpose potting mixture for average houseplants. And you haven't fainted yet! In fact, we'll bet you're feeling pretty good right now because you see there's no threateningly long list of bizarre ingredients that will launch you on an unforgettable wild-goose chase all over the country. And there's no ridiculous marathon "pot up" session that will consume five exhausting days as you switch from one soil mixture to another to another! Here all you have to deal with is three readily available, simple ingredients.

"But how much of each ingredient do I use?" you're asking, perhaps suspecting that this is the snare, where things get complicated again. Well, unfurrow your brow because it couldn't be easier. You use *one part of each ingredient*. That is, you use one part soil to one part peat moss to one part perlite (or sand or vermiculite). Let us put it another way: If you had three empty milk containers, you'd fill each container with one of the ingredients, so you'd have one container of soil, one container of peat moss, and one of, say, perlite. You dump the contents of all three containers into a receptacle, swirl them around a few times to mix them together well, and you've got it. Your handmade perfect potting soil is ready.

What happens, you may ask, if you don't mix enough? What happens if you mix too much? Not to worry! If you run out of mixture in the middle of potting up a plant, just mix up some more. Maybe this time fill the containers only one-fourth of the way. Should you mix up too much, just dump the extra in a plastic bag and tie a knot at the top. Then you'll have it ready for the next time. This procedure is so simple that by the second time around you'll have a good feel for how much to mix and probably have it down to a fine art. The formula is that easy. We've knocked out the frustration factor at every turn.

Let's go back for a moment to the bags of Wonder Mix stashed under the sink. Is this dirt utterly useless? To add insult to injury, are we telling you that you wasted your money? No, we are not. We're telling you that the problem with commercial mixes is that they are composed mainly of straight soil, with a meager sprinkling of perlite or vermiculite, and maybe all of a dash or two of peat moss. This 99 percent soil content is why the mixture turns into a hard brick when dry, turns into a swamp when wet, looks so dark and feels so heavy—and *is* too heavy for your plants. But you can use these Brand X mixes in our simple formula for exactly what they are—a bag of dirt. Add an equal part of peat moss and an equal part of, say, perlite. Both these ingredients "lighten" the soil and provide good moisture retention, yet aid in effective drainage. So one way or another, you've still got your proper potting soil that makes for happy, healthy roots, which grow happy, healthy plants.

This "one to one to one" mix is, by the way, the very same potting mixture that we at The Village Green have been serving up for some twelve years now. We're known far and wide for our soil. Every week we bag up the three ingredients in mountains of five-pound plastic bags. Our steady customers line up for the stuff. God help us when we run out on a busy Saturday morning; the corners of a lot of mouths go down fast, and raw disappointment fills the air. Why? Because it works! We know it, our customers know it, and soon you'll know it too.

By the way, we don't mix our soil because our customers can't do it. We simply provide the service to those who want the five pounds straight and fast. Some people, although in the minority, always request bags of the separate ingredients to do the measuring and mixing themselves. They enjoy it. Mixing a bag of the good earth is a soothing, pleasant, productive experience. So there it is. Our golden formula potting mixture is yours for the making. It's fun, it's easy, and it *works*.

Now, there may be more than a few of you staring forlornly at what used to be a nice little plant whose steady (or fast) decline was caused by roots locked into that "brick-swamp" soil base. And you're asking, "Is this it? Is there nothing I can do for this plant *now*?" The answer is yes, but not without considerable risk. In other words, you can change the soil around a plant's roots, but while it may be a tedious procedure for you, it is far tougher on the plant.

This total soil change is no picnic. It's not like handing your ailing plant a little miracle pill and presto! all is fine and dandy with a guaranteed smiling prognosis for the future. This radical total soil change is a touch-and-go, finicky business resorted to only when the known hazards of keeping the plant in that awful soil far outweigh the unknown risks of going for a dramatic change. So you go for broke, hoping the "cure" won't kill the plant.

What are the alternatives? Well, you can always do nothing and leave the plant in the grade Z soil in which it came, resigning yourself to its never-ending chronic ills that may eventually commend it to the deep anyway.

Or you can take the moderate position, the halfway solution that produces halfway results but may still save the plant. This way you wait for the next time the plant needs moving up to a larger pot and, without tampering with the roots in any way, you transplant it using the excellent potting soil extolled in this chapter. The net result is an old mediocre rootball surrounded by new fresh soil into which the roots will eventually venture. This way the plant is still better off than if you had continued to use "disaster soil," but it isn't as good as the plant whose roots are entirely immersed in a great soil. But you can live with that, and so can your plant.

One important footnote must be added to this procedure. Right from the start you must pack down the fluffy new soil to a density that approximates the hardness of the tightly wound rootball. Otherwise, when you water the plant, the new soil will absorb the water it needs and then drain ever so nicely, leaving that water-rejecting rootball as dry as a bone!

But if you need to take the risk of replacing all the soil, don't put it off. Do it now! Here's how. Water the soil thoroughly, and then gently ease the plant out of the pot. If gentle massaging causes some portions of the soil to fall away from the roots, that's good, you're ahead of the game. If, however, the roots have tightly wound themselves all around the soil, stop massaging and move on to part two. This is the harsh but inevitable part. Bring your plant to the sink with the drain in place and manipulate the faucet so that room-temperature water flows. Hold the plant under a force of water strong enough to wash away all the soil around the roots, but not so strong that you're blasting away at the helpless rootball. Continue this gentle washing away of soil for ten minutes, a half hour, or however long it takes until all you have in your hand is a pile of bare roots.

Immediately repot, using your new good soil. Hold the dangling root system in place and gently refill the pot with soil. Occasionally thump the pot (while still holding the root system in place with the other hand) to make sure that the soil falls down in place around all the roots. What we want is a pot full of roots and soil, with no large blank air pockets.

While entering the homestretch, note that the soil must come up on the stem at exactly the same point that it was before—no higher and no lower. When you're through, give the soil a thorough watering. And that's it—end of procedure.

But that's not the end of the story. Now, we wait. We wait in the ensuing days and weeks for our green patient to indicate its major discontent. It has, after all, undergone one of the horticultural world's more drastic life-saving procedures. However light and gifted the hand, roots are inevitably damaged, mashed, and lost to the drain. Our plant is not going to take this treatment lying down. What will it do? For starters, the plant will shed some leaves. How many? It's not easy to predict. If you're lucky, it'll lose only a few. But chances are we're talking about a lot more, perhaps a third of the foliage. Should matters take a serious turn for the worse, our plant may eliminate half its leaves, or there's always the possibility that it will lose all its leaves. Next, our plant may do something very predictable that's always guaranteed to give a good rousing scare: It may wilt. This tells us beyond a doubt that the root system is most unhappy and flashing the red lights. Last on our scale of escalating symptoms is the one thing we tried so hard to prevent: The plant may die.

That about covers the range of reactions our plant may

demonstrate. The question is, What can you do? Well, whatever happens, our number-one rule always is: Don't panic! Don't do something foolish such as apply fertilizer. Those roots are in no condition to handle a feeding. If our plant is losing an alarming number of leaves or if it is showing even the slightest wilt (a condition pointing to termination), it is clearly time to grab the pruning shears and start cutting back some of the foliage. The theory here is to ease the burden on a root system obviously failing to absorb water by *reducing* the demand from the other end, the thirsty foliage. The hope is that, with the reprieve, the roots will recover fast enough to save the abbreviated plant.

How do you do it? If the plant is one whose leaves emanate from a central crown (such as an African violet or spider plant), the only way you can prune it is to cut off the expendable outer, older leaves, leaving intact the newer growth at the core of the crown. If the wilt is severe, you have no recourse but to snip more foliage off, even if you're ultimately left with two lonely leaves.

If the plant belongs to the vast majority of plants capable of branching (such as coleus, Wandering Jews, Scheffleras, and so forth), the procedure goes like this: For a moderate wilt, prune off the top one-fourth or one-third of the plant. If it's a drastic wilt that's looking you squarely in the eye, you have no choice but to cut *way* back, perhaps to within inches of the soil. If you're crying, "But my plant will look awful. There'll be nothing left of it!" we hasten to remind you that even a severely pruned plant looks better than a dead one.

What else can you do? You can try misting the plant several times a day. Or go several steps further and place the entire plant in an inflated clear-plastic bag to capitalize on the benefits of very high humidity. But do be sure to open the bag for an hour or two every day to let things dry out. The rest is a simple matter of administering a little tender loving care and thinking positive thoughts.

That's it! Admittedly, none of the alternatives to the problems created by Wonder Mix are great, but they're better than what you had ten minutes ago! So go for one of them, and good luck!

5.

How <u>Not</u> to Be Intimidated by Transplanting

Transplanting a houseplant is not as easy as stepping out of a size six shoe and into a size seven, but it isn't that much harder either. Yet few horticultural procedures seem to conjure up more fear and trepidation than this simple act of moving a plant out of one pot and into another. Even experienced devotees of houseplants—those not-uncommon folks who hold that a house devoid of plants is an inferior wasteland—approach this annual or biennial green rite of passage with trembling fingers and rattling pots.

Why such anxiety? We at The Village Green sympathize with the little old lady who has arthritic knuckles and needs a helping hand to move up her collection of African violets, and we jump to assist her. But what about all the rest of you able-bodied folks with athletic fingers, who come out of the woodwork on a busy Saturday morning with your top-heavy specimens bursting their pots? How is it that you'll wait on a line for our assistance, rather than attempt the move yourself? What's the story here?

The analogy is your perfectly competent friend having you come over every morning to open the can of catfood and feed the kitty because somewhere along the line the can opener became the enemy—the source of intimidation. Can openers don't have teeth, they don't bite. They're nice little gadgets that perform a simple, most critical task to perfection. Just try opening a can without one! But there it is—the irrational fear. It is the feeling that the act, the task, is somehow beyond you. So, my friends, it seems to be with transplanting your plants.

Where did the fear come from? Maybe the fault lies with those well-intentioned plant books showing lavish series of photographs with all these pairs of hands twisting and turning pots. Close by are lumps of fresh soil all ready to go. The whole scenario is aided and abetted by snappy captions that say, "Twist the pot, but be sure not to yank too hard." They advise, "Go ahead and smack the pot with a sledgehammer, but don't hit harder than a soft thud." They warn, "Don't let the plant plop out, for heaven's sake, but don't be afraid of it either." Then they encourage: "Be aggressive but gentle. Have confidence but be careful."

So you study all this in deadly earnestness and try a move or two on an empty dummy pot, but by picture #2 you decide you'd rather have a tooth pulled than proceed further. Typically, you now do one of three things. You say, "The hell with it!" Then you drag the plant back to your others, all so top-heavy in tiny pots that one good sneeze could topple the entire collection.

Or you get creative. You look at your overgrown plant, whose roots are crammed into a pot so small that no way does it have a large enough base to hold itself upright. You say, "Okay! I cannot handle transplanting this thing, but I *can* play 'home engineer.' " So you look around the house for strange mismatched odds and ends to support your teetering plant through yet another year of life in the minipot. (See photograph 11.) What do you find? Why, lots of things! You find a dirty old broomstick and shove that into the soil, reinforcing it with an old wooden yardstick for the other side of the pot. Next you stick in dozens of yellow pencils to hold up the other parts of the plant that are helplessly flopping over the rim of the pot. All of these wonderfully coordinated supports you artfully tie together with reams and reams of string, reinforced with little bows here and large bulbous knots there. Around and around you go, until finally the green of your plant is almost totally obscured by a cocoon of white string that looks like the handiwork of a large deranged spider. "There!" you cry, cinching the last knot tightly. "That should do it." You fall back exhausted on the sofa, confident that you've solved today's problem and once more delayed Judgment Day.

Last on our list of typical solutions, you do what the majority of less inventive customers do: You haul yourself and your toppling plant out of the house, down the street, and through the door of The Village Green (or a place like it). You walk quietly to the end of a line of other folks similarly encumbered with overgrown, underpotted plants falling out of shopping bags and await salvation for your plant and your frustrations.

We ask you, What is all this nonsense? Sure, we at The Village Green are happy to have your business become our business. We can untie your knots and bows and extricate your plants from the pencils and broomsticks, Scotch tape, string and twistems, and from all those years of neglect. But truthfully, we'd rather take our time and your money for those procedures that are truly beyond your expertise and ability. Our business is plants, not phobias!

So let's see if right here and now we can break down and eliminate once and for all the "pot-up phobia" that has you tiptoeing through your plants with bated breath. Let's get rid of the fear that keeps you in the business of string collecting and broomstick hoarding, and that has reduced your once lovely plants to bizarre props for a junkyard jungle odyssey. Keep an open mind, and here goes.

First, let's start with the basics: What are the reasons for transplanting a plant? The reasons are *not* because you "feel like it," because you think the plant "might like it," because you think it "might be time." Barring the accident that has a plant shatter its pot, we transplant plants *when and as they need it*.

When do plants need to be transplanted? There are several indications. The first and most obvious clue does not require X-ray vision. Very simply, a plant needs transplanting when it looks ridiculously large in relation to its pot. This is the stage previously referred to in which the specimen is so top-heavy that it literally keeps falling over. (See photograph 12.) This is also the stage that finds your frustration quota soaring. Why does the plant refuse to support its weight? It is not because it wants to thwart your efforts at upright greenery. It is because the laws of gravity dictate that a plant must have a base (pot plus soil) sufficient in weight, size, and shape to enable that plant to maintain its upright position. Unless severely handicapped, a plant will continue to increase in size even after its base is too small for it. Eventually the weight of the plant above the soil line will determine its inevitable toppling. This is no act of volition, it is raw cause and effect in action.

While we're recalling Newton's contribution to physics, let's pause to examine what happens to a real-life plant stuck in tiny fairy-tale Cinderella shoes. We're not talking about mild crankiness because we can't go to the ball. Tiny pots sooner or later perpetrate real hardship on the living plant trapped in them. For starters, it is virtually impossible to properly water a severely pot-bound plant. Years ago its roots explored and exhausted every ounce of soil in that pot. Today its rootball consists of 98 percent roots and 2 percent soil. That 2 percent soil can't possibly hold water long enough for the roots to absorb it. Therefore, the water rushes right through the pot, leaving the plant every bit as parched as it was before the flash flood.

So how do you water such a plant? Forget about top watering. The only way to achieve anything remotely resembling a decent watering is to apply the thorough-soak-saucer method as detailed in chapter 3.

But now we face another problem—the issue of nutrition, as in sustenance, food. As the following chapter explains, water unlocks and makes available to a plant the nutrients contained in the soil. But a severely pot-bound plant will not receive any nutrients at watering time because, once again, there isn't enough soil in the first place to provide these nutrients.

What we have in the instance of a very pot-bound plant is a case of starvation. What can you do about it? Well, the best solution is to give some thought to the predicament of your green friend who can't do it himself, and *transplant the critter*, thereby providing him with all the necessary nutrients contained in the new soil. (In time and also in season you will eventually also supply fertilizer, as the following chapter explains.)

"Okay," you say, "I'm willing, but both my arms are broken and in casts. And all my friends who might help me transplant my plants have gone to Europe for the summer. Is there anything I can do for my plants until help arrives?" Yes, there is. Assuming that your legs aren't broken too, you can take yourself out the door to the nearest plant shop. There you can purchase a container of water-soluble fertilizer. And don't put it off for one more day.

What will the fertilizer do? It will give your plants the "something to grow on" that the absent soil can't.

Now please don't believe that a little can of Miracle Gro is the answer to your dreams—or nightmares! Don't think that you'll never have to face transplanting a plant again. The application of water-soluble and *highly diluted* plant food to a pot-bound plant is only a stopgap measure. This is a tide-you-and-your-plants-over tactic that you may resort to until your casts come off or your friends return from abroad.

What else happens to the pot-bound plant? Unless you follow the above, overgrown plants in tiny pots start to do some pretty sad things. Growth will be weak and spindly. New leaves will get smaller and smaller. Solid green leaves will become paler and paler. In plants capable of color, the plant simply does not have the fuel to maintain the rainbow effect and reverts more and more to plain green. And you can just forget about any blossoms from your flowering plants. One way or another, we're talking about a disadvantaged plant whose growth is stunted and deformed. As the weeks and months of hardship turn into years, the plant will one day simply stop growing altogether.

Do you want to really understand the dynamics here?

Then imagine or recall the last time you went without breakfast, lunch, and dinner. Do you remember that weak, limp feeling? Do you remember how the desire to walk another step faded from your heart? How just negotiating a street curb presented a major challenge? How jittery and nervous you were, and unable to manage yourself? Then you understand very well.

Now that we've given your former complacency a good shake—and gotten your attention—let's talk about the less drastic, more average signs. These are the ones your everyday, moderately root-bound plant will use to say, on a more friendly note, "It's time!" What are they? The classic familiar sign is the presence of roots emerging from the drainage holes of a pot. Now we don't mean one lonesome, wayward root that accidentally wanders out the basement door. We mean several roots pouring out. (See photograph 13.)

Still not sure? Then let's take a closer look. Wait until the next time this plant is due for a watering. After its soil is properly soaked, gently ease the rootball out of the pot. Look at it. Is there nary a root to be seen? Are you looking at solid brown soil? If the answer is yes, gently lower the rootball back into the pot, and rest assured that it's not time yet. If, however, lots of roots are clearly visible, the plant is ready. Needless to say, the unfortunate condition where roots have wound themselves around and around in a hard circle and where hardly any soil is visible signals a certified candidate for immediate transplanting.

Are there any other clearly visible signs that suggest "It's time"? Yes, we have one, last, most dependable indication that Moving Day is upon us. This one will help you determine the story with your medium-sized plants and heavy floor-sized monsters, whose rootballs are not so easily examined in a split-second popping off and on of a pot. With these big guys, what you survey is the clearly visible soil surface. You're looking for the presence of a fine webbing of roots at the soil's surface. (See photograph 13.) This tells us something very important: With the passage of time in the same pot, the root system rolled around and grew into and throughout the soil. With nowhere else to go, the roots turned upward to emerge at the surface of the soil. If the roots are there in any numbers, make no mistake about it— this is a loud "It's time!" If you don't see any roots, chances may be you're okay for a while.

At this juncture we want to draw a very clear distinction between the fine network just described and the presence of "aerial" roots. Aerial roots are those thick, fleshy roots that emerge from the base and along the stems of plants; they appear on plants as common as the philodendrons and on several of the epiphytic succulents, not to mention their prodigious presence on many orchids. The point is that these aerial roots are a root system separate and distinct from the "normal" root system under the soil. These aerial roots absorb water (and when present, nutrients) from moist air. They also serve to anchor the plant in whatever it happens to be growing in or on.

A familiar case in point that you've probably seen a hundred times is the philodendron merrily growing up that slab of wood. The regular root system, as we said, is under the soil just like any other plant. But if you'd taken a closer look at what was happening with the rest of this plant, you might have noticed thick, white (and sometimes barky) roots all along the stem anchoring the plant onto the wood slab. The presence of these aerial roots hardly indicates that this philodendron is pot-bound. These are aerial roots quietly and efficiently doing their job. But if you suspect that this plant is in need of a larger home, what do you do? Look for fine roots at the soil's surface. Check the drainage holes. Last, ease the rootball out of the pot and take a closer look.

Before we move on we want to draw one final distinction between what looks to the uneducated eye like "It's time!" and the actual fact. This concerns the unique case of cacti and succulents. These plants, unlike regular foliage plants, exhibit the phenomenon of sporting very small root systems relative to "all that plant" above the soil line. Is there something wrong here? Hardly. This is the nature of the beast. This minimal root system is designed by Nature to maximize the fast absorption of infrequent rains. For our purposes, do not look at our green friend from the desert in what appears to be a very small pot and automatically yell, "Cruelty! Neglect! How awful!"

Cacti and succulents are grown in these smaller pots because they have smaller root systems. Were you to pot them with the same aesthetics and practical theory reserved for "regular" plants, you would be setting them up for disaster. How so? Pot these plants in a bigger pot, with all that new soil surrounding those miniroot systems, and you'll promptly rot out the roots. On the other hand, if your cactus or succulent is bursting out of its pot or if it is constantly falling over, the weight of the plant above the soil line *has* exceeded the weight of its base (pot plus soil). This plant is ready for a larger pot!

Okay. Now that you understand the basics of when

to and when not to transplant, you're ready for the "how to." So here you are. You're staring at a plant that has passed at least one test that tells you "It's time!" Where do you go from here? From here you go into pots. But which ones? And how much larger? What about the clay-versus-plastic issue? Feeling overwhelmed? Don't— it's all infinitely logical.

First we have the how-big-a-move-up question. Is there a general rule of thumb here? Most certainly—you move up two inches. If your pot-bound friend is currently residing in a four-inch pot, it moves into a six-inch. If it's in a five-inch, we're talking about a seven-inch pot, and so on.

Are there any exceptions? Of course there are. There is the very big exception of the plant grown in the ubiquitous "grower's can" and destined for a clay pot. The reason we immediately contradict the rule of going up two inches is that the vast majority of medium and large plants that find their way to the florists and garden shops across the nation are grown in these very same straight-up-and-down plastic containers. If you will recall, the shape of a clay pot is not straight up and down but tapered. That is, while its top rim diameter may measure eight inches, its base diameter has slimmed down to a mere five inches. So if your transplant is the common one where you're going from grower's can into clay (or any other tapered pot), you must make allowance for the smaller base. Therefore, go for an increase in the top rim diameter of three inches and, in some rare instances, maybe even four inches. For example, if the top rim diameter of a grower's can measures five inches, choose a clay pot with a rim diameter of eight or nine inches.

Speaking of clay pots, you may have noticed that these pots are available in three shapes. There's the "standard" pot I'm sure you're all familiar with that comes in diameters as small as two-and-a-half inches all the way to seventeen inches. There's also the so-called azalea pot that comes in the same top rim diameters but is shorter and squatter. Then we have the even squatter "bulb" pot that is even closer to the ground.

What do we make of these shapes? For starters, they are certainly no reason for anxiety. These three pots simply allow you to choose the shape most appropriate to the nature of a particular plant's root system. Take the case of many of the begonias. These plants have a shallow root system that, rather than growing downward, tends to spread out laterally. Therefore, a shallow azalea pot or even the very squat bulb pot is very much in keeping with the nature of this root system that doesn't need and doesn't want additional depth to its pot.

The minimal root systems of cacti and succulents not

Three shapes of pots to choose from: the "standard," the "azalea," the "bulb"

only look great in these azalea and bulb pots but once again benefit from them. Why? A shallow pot that holds less soil holds less water, which means it is more difficult for you to flood these easily rotted root systems! So there they are. Real, concrete, practical reasons for choosing one shape over another.

You've got lots of other choices out there too. Take the clay-versus-plastic debate, for some a burning controversy. We say relax and let reason and your own sense of aesthetics dictate your choice. To help you make your decisions, let's look briefly at the properties of clay and plastic to appreciate the advantages and disadvantages of each.

Let's start with the issue of weight. Clay pots weigh more than their plastic counterparts. So what? Well, for instance, a tall, heavy, upright cactus will fare far better in a clay pot with some weight to it. Were you to put this same bulky fellow in a plastic pot of the same diameter and shape, it would be so top-heavy that it would literally spend half its life falling over. So clay is clearly dictated here. It is the perfect choice. It's a lifesaver for you and your plant.

Let's look at another situation: You have these lovely lightweight wooden shelves in your kitchen window that will bear only so many pounds. What is the obvious choice here in pots? Lightweight plastic. Along the same line, why are millions of hanging pots primarily manufactured in plastic and only a small percentage produced in heavyweight ceramic? Because all the ceilings and window moldings in the nation would promptly cave in were all those millions of hanging plants housed in anything but plastic.

Now let's address the always interesting watering issue.

Are you one who just can't seem to enjoy what for others is the pleasant task of watering plants? Then, barring those plants whose shape and bulk belong in a weighty terra-cotta pot, the plastic pot is obviously for you. It retains water and prevents evaporation from the sides of the pot 100 percent more effectively than a porous clay pot.

But maybe you have the reverse problem? Despite what you now know about when to water plants, do you practically have to tie yourself to the sofa to resist the urge to overwater them? Then, barring those specific situations that call for lightweight plastic, the answer to your problem is the clay pot. Why? Because it is porous. Excess water will quickly be drawn from the soil to the porous walls of the pot, easily and rapidly evaporating from there into the air. You could correctly water a plant in clay a good five times as often as its counterpart in plastic.

One could go on and on extolling the virtues and detractions of clay and plastic, but suffice it to say that after practical considerations, the choice becomes a pleasant aesthetic one. Some people would rather die than have anything but the traditional terra-cotta pot in their home. Other people love the choice of colors, textures, and shapes offered in plastic.

We'd like to say a serious word about the cachepot or decorative ceramic pot *that has no drainage holes*. Many of you insist upon placing your valuable plants into these containers because they're "decorative, pretty," and you can find ones to "match your decor." Well, while these pots may do wonders to upgrade your decor, they can also be a perfect *disaster* for your plants. Why? Excess water not needed by the plant collects at the bottom of the pot, thereby rotting the plant's roots. But if you insist upon using them, at least choose pots large enough so that you can stand your plant on a good base of pebbles well *above* the waterline when the inevitable floods occur. But even so, watch these cachepots like a hawk!

Now the matter of to crock or not to crock. "Crocking" is the act of placing a few shards (pieces of broken old clay pots) or medium-sized pebbles over the drainage holes of a pot in such a way as to prevent the escape of soil when watering. But it still allows excess water to drain out and away. Generally speaking, one does not bother to crock pots whose diameters are less than six inches, unless you are deliberately seeking to weigh down a plant that would otherwise be top-heavy. As you get into larger sized pots, however, crocking is generally an excellent idea.

Okay. With your pots and crocks in order, it's time to learn when not to and when to transplant a plant. It goes like this: Don't transplant during the winter months. Generally speaking, the months of November, December, and January will find your houseplants taking their annual rest, their pause, their vacation from active growth. This is also the time of year when the daylight hours are shorter and the sun's rays are weaker. Add to this natural calendar the hardship perpetrated by the dry, desertlike humidity in the average home created by central heating. It is no wonder then that the average houseplant knows what it's doing when it says, "Forget about sending up a new leaf or two now. These conditions are terrible. Think I'll sit tight for a while and wait until spring for a little action." That's just about what it does. It sits tight, simply maintaining its present size, hoping to somehow survive the adverse winter conditions, to rear its little head again along about February or March when the environment is more conducive to its needs.

What does this tell you? It says forget about transplanting in November. Put December out of your mind altogether. The bottom line here is that we have a dormant plant with a slumbering root system that won't venture so much as an exploratory root hair into any fresh soil until early spring. To ignore this hibernation and transplant anyway will set your plants up for a riproaring case of root rot. That new soil will hold and retain quantities of water that not only is of no use to the roots but is lethal to them! It will rot them as they sleep.

When should you think "transplant time"? Think about it in the spring and summer months, which means from February all the way to October. This is when your plants are actively awake and growing. If we really want to get exact about it, think February, March, and April. These early spring months will catch your plants right at that point where they are just awakening from their winter rest and are ready to have a go at some real growth. So this is the ideal point to move the plant up into that needed larger pot.

Perhaps you're now wondering: "Is there any harm done if I forego the spring transplant and do my pot-ups in the summer months?" The answer is certainly not. As indicated, plants are in their active growth cycle from February all the way to October. A transplant anytime during this period is fine and dandy, and infinitely better than the ill-advised November move-up. Just be aware that a late transplant in, say, June, will interrupt the concentration of a plant focused on new growth as it pauses to adjust and recover from the move. But that's okay because in a matter of weeks it will resume the business of new growth and continue merrily on until the fall, when its inner clock and the calendar once more say, "Slow down. The season is drawing to a close. It's time to get ready to rest."

Okay. You've gotten the when to's and the when not to's and the why's and the wherefore's of the transplant story. Now you're ready for the simplest, most rewarding part of all: the actual "how to." So let's get to it. You've got your pot-bound plant sitting in front of you. You've chosen an appropriate pot. Next to that you've got your fresh soil all set to go.

Your first challenge is how to get the plant out of the old pot. At this first step many books will already be avidly suggesting that you hold your plant upside down and start thumping the pot against a hard surface, at the same time cautioning you not to let that rootball flop out onto the floor (which it occasionally will do). Rather than resort to any gymnastics on anyone's part, we're going to direct you to leave your plant standing right where it is, and instead instruct you to give the stem(s) the lightest little tug to see what happens. Now we don't mean that mad, desperate yank you employ to disengage the suction of a plunger stuck on its target. We mean an effective but *gentle* tug on the stem(s) to see, literally, what gives. Nine times out of ten your plant will "give." The rootball lets loose from the sides and bottom of the pot and, presto, out it comes.

Let's say, for argument's sake, that the rootball isn't budging and that the pot we happen to be dealing with is a clay one in which roots have attached themselves to the walls. Now what? Now we escalate our tactic. Still keeping the plant right side up, get a knife (preferably a sharp one) from the kitchen. Run it all around where the rootball is glued to the sides of the pot. Having run it around once or twice, try the ease-up-and-out technique once again and give that gentle tug on the stem(s).

Almost always, the knife treatment does the job and the stubborn rootball pops out. But in order to cover all bases, we'll let the plot thicken. Let's say that the rootball still refuses to budge. Now what? Well, it would appear that our green friend doesn't know what's good for it. Here it is, its feet squeezed into this funny old pot, but it won't let go. Undaunted, we escalate our tactic to the next step. This doesn't mean hurl the plant, pot first, against the nearest wall. That is a sign of frustration and helplessness, and you feel neither. You are simply, calmly, and decisively sizing up a situation, and you're ready to shift gears when needed. The next gear calls for a good soaking for a half hour in a sink or tub. Every particle of soil and every pore of that clay pot should be saturated. If luck is with you, the water will loosen that rootball from the sides of the pot. Now try the knife procedure and a gentle tug again.

If this doesn't work, continue to remain calm and collected, scaring neither yourself nor your frightened plant, which is putting up quite an admirable struggle to keep things the way they are. It's time to resort to even more determined measures. Once again, this doesn't mean rush out the door in a heated frenzy and let the next bus that comes along run over the pot, a tactic guaranteed to dislodge more than the rootball from the pot. This means it's time to get clever. With your nerves calmly focused on outwitting the resistant rootball, you must shift to yet a higher gear. The higher gear, by the way, includes something every household has at least one of—a hammer! Now don't let fantastic visions of bludgeoning your plant to death leap around in your mind, fueled by thoughts of the last person who made you crazy with anger. Remember: This is your little green friend in the pot. This is the plant that kept you company through thick and thin, who sat up nights with you and has rewarded your efforts at indoor greenery. This plant has done everything it was supposed to do. Its only crime is that it is the net result of your former Pot-Up Phobia. It has grown attached to its tight shoes and is afraid to let go, so you're not going to shatter its shoes. You're simply going to offer some "encouragement." With the hammer in one hand and the pot in the other, and reassuring words for the plant in between, you are going to give that pot the nicest, lightest, little smack with the hammer. Go ahead and do it! Almost always, one smack will do it. The pot cracks and that's it. The rootball that moments ago was a prisoner is now free. If one smack doesn't do the trick, try another one. As you'll see, in a matter of minutes you're home free. You've got your overgrown rootball sitting in your hands and you're surveying a well-deserved sight that hasn't graced your eyes for years. (By the way, this exercise has also just provided a nice little supply of clay shards for future use.)

Let's go back and see what the story is for plants stuck in plastic pots. The procedure is exactly the same until the point where the rootball's determination to stay put caused household tools to appear that hadn't been seen for years. With plastic pots, the extra "persuasion" comes not with a hammer but in the form of a heavy-duty scissors or a nice pair of pliers. What do you do with them? You cut or pry, as the case may be, the pot away from the rootball. Do not do this as though your old hated gym teacher were breathing down your neck with a stopwatch! There is no audience here, no stopwatches, no prizes, no pressure. It's just you and your plant and the pliers or scissors, in the privacy of your own home. If it takes you five minutes, so be it. Let them be five directed, unhassled minutes. If you like to take your time, take the afternoon. The point is for you to keep your nerves intact, and for your plant to keep its roots intact. I suspect that if you're like most people instructed in this "take it easy and take your time" method, in a matter of mere minutes you'll be looking at a rootball that hasn't seen the light of day for years. Once again, you did it!

The rootball is now unencumbered; what do we do with it? Before we commend it to its just reward, the new roomy pot, we want to take this opportunity to see if it requires doctoring of any kind. Now don't get upset! The hard part is over. You got the rootball off, didn't you? We just want to take this well-deserved few minutes to check a few things. If old shards or other crocking material can be easily extricated, go ahead and remove them. Also, look at the whole of the root system. Are the visible roots brown with nice white tips? If so, things look good. If your survey reveals any soft, black areas, however, this is rot. These areas must be gently and carefully cut out with a sharp, clean knife. Now don't get all upset and excited. This isn't open-heart surgery. This is a matter of a snip or two on a rough, tough, overgrown rootball that ounce for ounce is probably stronger than you are. So grasp it firmly in hand, brace it against a hard surface, and go to it! Now, lest we leave in the dark anyone presented with a more serious problem, let's say that your examination uncovers large areas of rot and that you're apparently going to be doing a bit of unscheduled excavation. Still no reason for panic. The philosophy and procedure are the same. You're just doing ten snips to someone else's one.

An important point that we want to stress here is that if the rot has you snipping off something like one-third of your root system, then it is imperative that you prune off that same percentage of your plant's foliage. As chapter 8 discusses, we must always maintain that critical proportion of so many roots to so many leaves. So if the plant with the pruned roots is one where leaves grow out from a central crown, such as an African violet, simply snip off approximately one-third of its outer, older leaves. For plants capable of branching, such as a Schefflera, cut off the top one-third of the plant to match the one-third pruned roots. That's all there is to it.

Let's return to our rootball case study. If the roots are tightly wound around one another, see if you can ever so gently loosen up that situation. Don't go at it with an ice pick! Just gently massage the ball and let your gentle but effective prodding ease up that solid mass.

Having checked for all of the above and made any necessary corrections, our rootball is ready to move into its new home. If your pot is larger than six inches and you want to use crocking material, this is the time to put it in.

Eye the height of the rootball compared to the height of the pot. You can even give the new pot a try and place the rootball in it. The decision you want to make is how much or how little soil to place at the bottom of the pot so that, at the completion of the transplant, the surface of the rootball and the fresh soil will uniformly reside a good two inches below the rim of the new pot. This little determination is extremely important. If you add too much soil at the base, the transplanted plant will be at the same level as the rim of the pot. What will that do? It will make it virtually impossible to water this plant properly. With no space to gather and then seep down through the soil, the water simply rolls right off the top of the soil and splashes away. So if you value your nerves, don't commit this little mistake that you'll regret for years.

Setting the rootball too low in the pot won't drive you mad with frustration, but it doesn't look good. It looks bad. So set that rootball at the proper level right from the start!

Okay. With crock in place and X amount of soil over that, and the rootball nicely centered, it's time to add the rest of the soil. Are there any tricks of the trade here? Just a few. Occasionally thump your plant and new pot against a hard surface as you're filling in the soil so that it all falls down in place. We don't want large blank air pockets in here, just solid soil. When you're dealing with a very dense, tightly packed root system, it is most important that you *firmly* pack down your new soil to a hardness approxiating the density of the old rootball. Otherwise, when you water the plant in the future, water will drain perfectly through the new soil, bypassing that dense water-resistant rootball. So don't be afraid—pack that soil down to the necessary firmness.

As you're entering the homestretch, bear in mind that there is one exception to the rule that says the transplanted plant must have its new soil at exactly the same level as the surface of the old rootball. This is the instance referred to earlier in this chapter where we had that fine network of little roots at the soil's surface that told us this plant needed transplanting fast. These surface roots do *not* belong exposed to the air; they're supposed to be covered with soil. This is the time to cover those roots! The allotment of space for this "finishing" touch of soil in this specific situation is to be taken into consideration at the *beginning* of the transplant. And remember: With everything completed, the soil must still fall two inches below the rim of the pot.

Speaking of special instances involving roots, do *not* cover aerial roots that, as stated earlier, sometimes emerge at the base of the stem where it emerges from the soil. Aerial roots belong in the air! Along the same line, some plants, such as the popular fig trees, often send down from their trunks a maze of hard, barky "hold fast" roots that help to anchor the trunk to the ground. These roots, like aerial roots, also are not to be covered with soil.

Now an emphatic word about *not* fertilizing the newly transplanted plant. If, for whatever the reason, a pot-up must occur in the no-growth winter months, absolutely *no* fertilizer is applied until new growth begins in the spring. If the pot-up occurs at any time during the active spring and summer months, absolutely *no* fertilizer is applied for those couple of "adjustment" weeks following a transplant.

Now don't think for a moment that you're depriving your plant of sustenance. Even if the root system could handle it (which it can't), your fresh potting soil (see preceding chapter) more than fits the bill nutritionally. When the root system is feeling up for dinner, it will help itself to the bounty that is already there.

Last: the special case of cacti and succulents. These plants have roots that are tiny, slow-growing, and easily burned by fertilizer. No matter when the transplant, these plants must wait until the *following* spring for any application of plant food. Once again, not to worry. Their fresh soil will provide the "what to grow on" to carry them through the first season of growth.

What's left? A final, very satisfying, thorough watering of the soil. To achieve it, let the plant soak in water in the sink or tub for a half hour. Or put a waterproof saucer under the pot and water the soil. Excess water will eventually drain out to be reabsorbed. Then repeat the process until, a half hour later, you *know* you've done a thorough job. Allow the plant a few days in the shade before you move it back to its regular site. And that's it.

As you start to shed the grip of the Pot-Up Phobia that held your plants captive all these years, I'm sure you'll begin to see that this business of moving a plant from one pot to another is much like learning to ride a bicycle. At first it looks hard—it looks impossible!—but once you get the hang of it, it's a breeze. You may not be able to do it with your eyes closed, but you'll never forget how!

6.

How <u>Not</u> to Feed Big Dinners That Bring On Terminal Indigestion

or Less Is More with Fertilizing

It is an interesting phenomenon that while even avid plant lovers shy away from horticultural procedures, such as making up their own potting mixtures, and stampede at the mere thought of transplanting their plants, with fertilizing the opposite reaction reigns. It's love at first sight for the box of Miracle Gro and instant affinity for the bottle of Rapid Grow. Not only is there no fear of buying and using plant food, but its use is something of a national pastime. It's a pastime that solidly and forthrightly equates a daily dose of fertilizer for your plants with an apple a day for you. As though that weren't bad enough, there pervades a consummate belief that plant food will cure anything. It's a belief manifested everyday by customers who confidently stride over to the counter at The Village Green and say something like, "My plant is dropping leaves. I need to get vitamins for it." Or, "The dog knocked over my philodendron, and it looks bad. What kind of fertilizer do you have?" Then there's the customer who cries, "My neighbor really destroyed my plants while I was away, and they're all dying. I need some fertilizer!" As a matter of fact, we have often said that if we could harness just 1 percent of this unbridled enthusiasm for fertilizing and apply it to the general resistance to, say, pruning, hundreds of rangy, overgrown, out-of-control plants could be transformed overnight into well-behaved beauties.

Let's look at this issue of fertilizing. Or is the issue *over*fertilizing? Let's see if we can separate myth from reality and in the process offer some suggestions about why, when, and how to use the different forms and formulas of fertilizer.

You may already be asking the following very logical question: Why fertilize at all if, as so enthusiastically described in chapter 4, a good potting soil is so terrifically nutritious for your plants in the first place? It's a good question. Here's the answer: It's true that a proper potting soil does supply excellent nutrition, but here's the catch—water "unlocks" the nutrients in soil. It does this by dissolving the nutrients in a solution, thereby making them available and palatable to a plant's roots. This is a fact we willingly and happily accept. The problem is that with each and every watering most of that nutritional soup ends up washing right out the drainage hole, never to be seen again, thereby slowly but surely depleting the soil. If our plant were merrily growing in the fertile ground of a tropical forest, there would be no problem. The natural cycle of animal and plant matter living, dying, and decomposing nearby would present our hungry plant with a never-ending abundant supply of nutrients. But our plant isn't growing in the jungle. It lives in the very close-ended artificial unit of a pot on your windowsill, watching its nutrients leach away with every watering. This is why we fertilize.

With this understanding under your belt, let's talk fertilizers. As you may already be aware, plant food comes in various forms. The generally familiar ones are the liquids that are diluted with water, the powders that are mixed with water, fertilizer stakes that are pushed down into the soil, and time-release food pellets that are added to the soil. Then there are the various, less familiar "organic" fertilizers such as dried cow manure, dried blood, bonemeal, and the like, which can be added to the potting soil or later scratched into the surface of the soil.

We realize that your fertilizing habit may well be the usual one where you walk into shops such as ours and walk out with your old familiar brand in the yellow box. And that's about as far as it goes. Your old tried-and-true choice of plant food may well be the perfect choice for you. But let's make sure you know what you're buying.

Have you ever "read" a box of plant food? No, we don't mean just the manufacturer's recommendations for use. We mean that funny set of three numbers separated by dashes that all fertilizers must have displayed somewhere on the container. You probably glossed over these or found them annoying because you didn't know what to make of them. Maybe you never even noticed them, an oversight for which you're hardly to be blamed. All of us tend to automatically dismiss from thought that which is unfamiliar, particularly if it seems to be of little consequence anyhow. And surely three little numbers on a container for which no meaningful explanation whatsoever is ever offered would fall into this category of "instant oblivion." But we're here to tell you that these three numbers are indeed of consequence. Their significance is well within your grasp, and an understanding of them as they relate to your particular collection of plants is well worth the easy effort.

What are these numbers that typically read something like 15–30–15, 30–10–10, 0–7–1, or whatever else? These numbers stand for the three major elements of plant nutrition. Reading from left to right, the first number stands for nitrogen (N.), the middle number for phosphorus (P.), and the last for potassium (K.). Their representation in the three-figured formula tells you the percentages of these elements contained in the particular plant food you're considering. So, a very common fertilizer formula such as 15–30–15 represents 15 percent nitrogen, 30 percent phosphorus, and 15 percent potassium. You will notice that these elements add up to only 60 percent, not the anticipated 100 percent. The remaining 40 percent is made up of a tiny percentage of trace elements and then nonfood filler. Both of these figures are often indicated somewhere in small print on the back of the container. Filler and minute trace elements aside, it is that three-figured formula on the front of the container that we want to focus on.

For the purposes of the indoor gardener, all fertilizers can be divided into two main categories—those for green foliage plants, and those for flowering plants or plants that sport colors other than green. If you have a collection of nonflowering green plants, this is the formula approach to take: Look for the plant food with a high-nitrogen number. How would that formula read? Remembering that the first number on the left is nitrogen, it would read something like 30–10–10 or 10–5–5 or 9–2–1. You'll notice that *all* these formulas have a high-nitrogen content relative to the smaller percentages of phosphorus and potassium. That high nitrogen promotes good green growth.

What's the story for your flowering plants and plants of color? This time we want a formula higher in the middle number, which is phosphorus, the element that promotes quality flower production. (Phosphorus also promotes robust roots.) We're now talking a 15–30–15 formula or 5–10–5 or 1–5–2.

Because potassium, the last element, also encourages good flower production (in addition to building overall sturdiness and disease resistance), a formula that reads something like 15–30–30 or 5–10–10 is also excellent for flowering and colorful plants.

You may have observed that some of the formulas have higher numbers and others lower numbers. What's the difference between them? The difference is simply that a higher numbered fertilizer such as 15–30–15 is stronger than 5–10–5. Later on we'll talk about stronger versus weaker. For now, simply understand that any one of these high-phosphorus or high-phosphorus-bolstered-by-high-potassium formulas would fill the bill for your flowering plants.

Now that you understand the fertilizer formula story, let's discuss when to use them. Is it complicated? Not at all. *Fertilize plants when and as they need it.* When do they need it? They need it when they are actively growing during the spring and summer months. This means you should start fertilizing in February or March and continue all the way through October. See? As promised, it couldn't be simpler or more logical.

Here, however, are some exceptions of sorts. If you're lucky enough to have great growing conditions for your plants, such as the bright, moist environment created in a glass-enclosed garden room, you will find that the active growing season for your plants is remarkably extended. That is, it starts earlier in the spring and lasts well into the fall. In this event, your fertilizing regime should fall in line, starting earlier and lasting longer.

Similarly, if you are fortunate enough to have a home greenhouse, the long growing season is even further extended. That is, while the rest of the indoor green world is still fast asleep and your envious neighbors in their dark, dry apartments are struggling just to keep their dormant plants alive, for you spring has sprung! Ignore the fact that the calendar says it's only January 2. Your plants are starting to jump out of their pots, and their subsequent lavish growth will continue to reflect the ideal environment of a greenhouse. So what do you do with your fertilizer? You follow suit and use it!

But for the rest of us ordinary folk, we dark apartment dwellers and possessors of average to poor growing situations who make up the bulk of indoor gardeners, make no mistake about it! Spring starts along about February or March and ends around October, and that's it!

Now that you have some understanding of when to fertilize, let's go to the flip side, every bit as important—when *not* to fertilize. We began this chapter describing plant food as the popular "snake oil" preparation of the 80's. Why? Not because fertilizing isn't an excellent idea but because what permeates this land is the idea that vitamins for plants will cure everything. The numbers of true believers are even increasing. No matter what it is—overwatering, underwatering, too big a pot, too small a pot, the cat had an accident in the pot, cold, heat, bugs, blight, mold, fungus—the popular myth is that a good dose of fertilizer will fix it. People believe that it will reverse the overwatering, make a big pot small, make a small pot big, neutralize what the kitty did, make the cold hot, make the hot cold, kill the bugs, wipe out the mold, and on and on and on. If such a miraculous concoction existed, we'd all be sitting pretty amid our own Gardens of Eden, picture-perfect in every detail.

But this is not how fertilizer works. This is how a myth works. Fertilizer does one very important thing and one thing only: It provides food to plants. And its gross misuse, which includes not just why but when and how it's used, places it as the number-two killer of houseplants. (Overwatering is number one.) So "cure-all" is hardly the case. When misused, the term "kill-all" is more like it.

What constitutes misuse of plant food?

Number One: fertilizing during the winter months. As you may recall from previous chapters, the months of November, December, and January find your plants inactive, dormant, "asleep." They need and want to rest from the previous spring and summer's active growth. To blithely ignore this fact and feed them anyway is like poking a hibernating bear in the rear. Your plants will not bite back or try to kill you, but we assure you that any artificial growth stimulated by your plant food is not going to be lovely. It is going to be weak and spindly and perfectly awful.

Number Two: As already indicated, plant food does *not* cure an overwatered plant. A damaged, rotting root system has all it can do just trying to stay alive. So not only is fertilizing at this point absolutely pointless, *it is lethal!* When can you fertilize an overwatered plant? Only *after* it has recovered. How will you know? Assuming all evidence of damage has ceased (see chapter 3) you'll know for certain you're in the clear at the moment your plant starts to send out new growth. At this point, providing also that the calendar reads those nice spring and summer months, you may resume or commence your season of fertilizing.

Number Three: As we discussed in the preceding chapter on transplanting, we do *not* fertilize plants that are recently transplanted. Wait the customary two to three weeks. Cacti and succulents must wait until the following spring.

Number Four: To believe and then act upon the recommended dosage on so many commercial fertilizers constitutes a misuse nine times out of ten. How so? Manufacturers understandably want to sell their product. They want you to use it, run out of it, and then go back and buy more. This might be fine and dandy if you owned stock in the fertilizer company. But the recommended dosage on almost every single brand of plant food is *far too strong* for the average houseplant that is caught in the less-than-ideal conditions with which most of us struggle. So if you take those instructions as gospel, know that you're committing the sin of overfertilizing.

Now don't misunderstand us. If your philodendron were happily basking in a Brazilian jungle, we'd be the first ones to say, "Sure, go ahead. Feed at the recommended dosage. Have a plant food party!" Those conditions couldn't be better to support that kind of "speed" growth. The light is there, there's that nice drop in temperature at night, the humidity couldn't be higher, the air circulation couldn't be better, and the scenery isn't bad either. The same goes for those of you whose plant environments are greenhouses and garden rooms and sun porches.

But let's return to the black-and-white reality that 99 percent of houseplants are not grown in heaven. They're grown in houses and apartments like yours and mine. Therefore, it is imperative that we do something to slow down these ninety-mile-an-hour "jungle perfect" plant food formulas to render them safe and appropriate for our plants which live in the "real" world. What can we do? Take our motto at The Village Green that says, "Less is more," and *dilute way down*. If your favorite brand of liquid fertilizer says use ten drops per gallon of water, forget that nonsense and use five. If your brand of plant food stakes says use five of these things for a particular size pot, use two. If some label suggests that you use three tablespoons of time-release pellets for one-fourth bushel of soil, use one. And so on and so on and so on.

We'd like to pause for a moment and comment on what twelve years of experience at The Village Green has taught us and what has been revealed to us in garden shops and supermarkets around this land: By far the public's number-one choice of plant food is none other than the ever-popular water-soluble powder plant food. You know these fertilizers. They turn the water a dazzling turquoise. While some brand names guarantee "miracles," others say that "rapid growth" is what you can expect, but whatever they call themselves and whatever their promises, these plant foods are the preparation of your choice. It is a choice we heartily endorse. Unlike hit-and-miss stakes and pellets and other things, with these water-soluble fertilizers you can carefully control exactly what your plant is getting. So we say by all means use them, but *not* at the recommended two- or four-week intervals. That is like shoving Thanksgiving dinner down your plant's throat one week, starving it for a few weeks, then emptying the refrigerator on its plate again, and then having it go without food again! This is no way to feed a plant. This is feast or famine!

The secret to nonjolting, perfect, even fertilizing is to use it every time you water throughout the spring and summer months, but hardly at the recommended dosage. The idea is to use just enough powder—a dash, two dashes—to barely tint the water. This feed-as-you-water technique could not be more palatable or more suited or more appreciated by your plants. The beauty is that you aren't restricted to the major annoyance of having to mix up a gallon or bathtubful of the stuff to get the dilution right. And you don't have to think in terms of quarts and pints and tablespoons and teaspoons. Whatever you water with, be it a two-quart watering can or a teacup, you simply drop in however many pinches of blue powder necessary to give the water that ever-so-slight tint. And that's it! No strange concoctions to store. No waste. No hit-and-miss. No nothing! *You can't miss.*

Before we leave the land of hungry plants, let's not forget those organic fertilizers, such as dried blood, bone meal, and cow manure. What are these substances, where do they come from, and how are they used?

We could spend the next five pages telling you how blood is collected at slaughterhouses, later dried and ground up to make dried blood, and that it is a perfectly acceptable source of nitrogen (and other elements) for your green foliage plants. We could tell you that bones are also collected at slaughterhouses, steamed to remove the fats, and then pulverized into a powder we call bone meal. We might add that this is a perfectly acceptable form of phosphorus (and other elements) for your flowering plants. We could then proceed to cow manure, whose origin is self-explanatory, and tell you that it's treated to cool down its burning properties, and then deodorized. Like bone meal, it's also a perfectly acceptable source of nutrients for your flowering plants.

If we were to conclude this brief dissertation on the merits and properties of these organic fertilizers, we'd tell you to choose the right one for your plants, use one-third or one-half the recommended dosage, and either add it to the regular ingredients of your good potting soil or later scratch it into the surface of your plant's soil. The problem is that we rarely get past the answer to the original question of where these fertilizers come from before even the most committed lover of houseplants is clutching his stomach, crying, "You mean they use blood, real blood?" The image of bones boiling around in a caldron also tends to be a conversation stopper. And forget about cow manure! No matter how much he values his precious plants and wants to do right by them, the average apartment and home dweller is not interested in toting even the smallest five-pound bag of this stuff past his doorstep. Why not? Ninety-nine percent of you indoor gardeners do not find these organic fertilizers acceptable in the slightest! You find them bulky, impractical, and sometimes frightening. Particularly for city dwellers, they conjure up visions of cows and bones and blood and waste products you're all perfectly happy to see stay on the farm. If it took you a good five years to accept bean sprouts on your plate, we suspect it'll take another five years for you to accept the merits of a little bone meal for your plants.

Therefore, rather than try to shove them down your

throat, let's leave these natural products to the folks who love them and avidly use them year in and year out. Who are these people? They're outdoor gardeners, the people with patios and decks and terraces and vegetable gardens and landscaped grounds. (And lots of work and storage space!) These folks would rather go on a diet themselves than give up cow manure for their tomato plants or bone meal for their bulbs or dried blood for their shrubs. These people swear by the results of their earthy fertilizers. And they're right!

On the other hand, if you're one of the brave, exceptional few who took to bean sprouts the same week they sprang on the scene, maybe you're also not put off by the earthiness of these animal product fertilizers, and you would like to incorporate them into the diet of your indoor greenery. Fine! As already stated, these fertilizers are excellent sources of nutrition for your plants. But they do have a few detractions for the indoor gardener. They are extremely slow and haphazard about releasing their nutritive value to the soil. For example, an application of, say, bone meal to the soil of a hungry plant in March is not going to find its way into your plant's system and won't do it the slightest bit of good until May. And we have no way of telling which week in May. By then, the active growth season for your plant is already half over! Therefore, circle the first week in January as the time to get that bone meal (or whatever) into or onto the soil so that by the time your plant is already actively growing in March, that bone meal will be well dissolved and doing its thing. Even so, you still have no way of knowing how much of the bone meal dissolved and how much is yet to dissolve. What you do know for sure is that the use of these organic fertilizers is a most imprecise science.

In addition, particularly for urbanites, these natural fertilizers are messy to use and messy to store. You get the feeling that, while they may be marvelous for your plants, somehow you've brought into your home more of the great outdoors than you had bargained for. Despite what the cheery sanitized label says, some users swear they can still smell the cows!

When all is said and done, our hearty recommendation to those of you for whom the word organic holds great appeal is this: Rather than use these hit-and-miss, who-knows-exactly-when-they-dissolve fertilizers as the main source of your plant's nutrition, use them *in addition to* the carefully controlled, evenly released, neat and clean water-soluble plant foods, whose food value is instantly available to your plants.

So there you have it. The in-season growth, the out-of-season rest, the "less is more," the "do it every time you water." These are the basic guidelines of how to feed your plants. You'll remember we began this chapter by telling you how "fertilizer happy" you are. It is our hope that we've toned you down and turned you and your plants around.

7.

How <u>Not</u> to Be Plagued by Insects and Other Bugs

Now don't get squeamish, but don't think you can duck this issue either! Neither high drama nor sticking your head in the sand is going to alter an immutable fact of indoor gardening life: Sooner or later, one way or another, the best (or worst) kept, the most treasured (or ignored), the most wonderful (or the most decrepit) houseplants are going to battle with that age-old despised pest, the indoor bug!

Perhaps you're one of the unlucky ones who knows too well that bugs strike plants. For years you've had to tentatively peer through generation upon generation of spray-resistant, tougher-than-nails, diehard insects just to find your meager indoor greenery. Whether you're new to the bug game or a seasoned hand, whether it's three measly mealy bugs or a veritable fleet you're fighting, take heart. Help is on the way. We'll show you how to look for bugs, how to identify the ones you have, which plants they tend to prefer, what they do to those plants, and last but not least, we'll show you what to do about them.

What's the first word on bugs? Prevention! It starts the moment you walk into a plant shop and pick up a plant. Right here, *before* you bring the plant home, you will inspect it for bugs. How do you do It? Start at the top of the plant and work your way down. Check the newest growth, check the upper and undersides of a leaf, check the joint where a leaf attaches to the stem, check the entire length of a stem, check the surface of the soil, then take a peek at the bottom of the pot. If this kind of inspection doesn't turn up any six- or eight-legged creatures lurking about, chances are good that the specimen in your hand is bug-free. However, a plant that passes the bug test in the shop is not automatically handed a clean bill of health. It can easily harbor bugs that slipped past you. Therefore, to be on the safe side and to protect your old plants from possible contagion, isolate this new plant for a couple of weeks after you bring it home. If it passes the test of time still bug-free, you and it are in the clear!

Next: Don't set up your plants for a big bug invasion by overwatering them. What's the connection? As you learned in chapter 3, an overwatered plant is a debilitated plant. Its roots are rotting, its stems are weak and spindly, its waterlogged leaves are yellowing and falling apart. In short, all structures and all systems are failing. Does this plant look good to a wandering bug looking to stake a claim somewhere? It looks great! The average bug knows better than to pick on a robust, healthy plant. A healthy plant is far too tough and sturdy to get a foothold on. The bug needs a sick overwatered plant on which it can get a stranglehold.

Next: Don't overfertilize plants! As you learned in the preceding chapter on fertilizing, overdoing it with the plant food not only doesn't help plants, it hurts them. In some cases it will kill them. Does an overfertilized plant with scorched leaves look good to a bug? You bet! It looks almost as good as an overwatered plant.

If you commit both mistakes—overwatering and over-fertilizing—on the same plant at the same time (which is common enough), you might as well stick a sign in the plant that reads: "Bugs: It's yours."

Last: As the following chapter on pruning will tell you, always prune off fading flowers, yellow leaves, or otherwise decomposing foliage before the bugs and blight find them. Pick up fallen leaves from the soil's surface. That little layer of debris creates a wonderful hiding and breeding ground for pesky little life forms to play under.

Does an ounce or two of bug prevention go a long way? You bet it does. It may keep you bug-free for years. But later, rather than sooner, some bug will find even your healthiest plant and set up house. What will you do about it? To conquer the enemy, you first have to know him. To help you know each of the bugs we will be discussing, we'll tell you in some detail how to recognize it, which plants it prefers, what it does to those plants, and what you can do about the bug.

Mealy Bugs

The three insects most commonly found on houseplants are mealy bugs, mites (by definition not an insect but an arachnid, like a spider), and scales. Let's take them in order. First, mealy bugs. These are small insects (thank God!), about one-fourth inch long at maturity. Their bodies are gray-white, oval, and are covered with a white, wooly, powdery wax. Now this insect is often mistaken

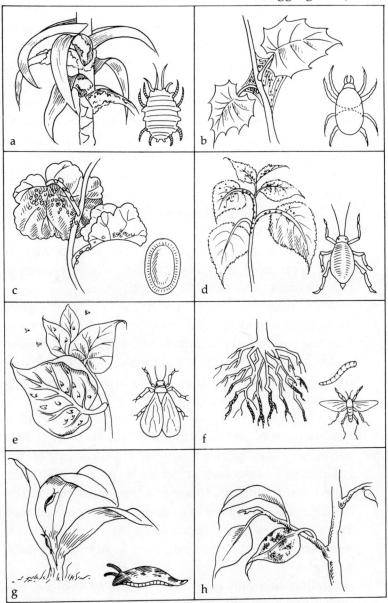

a) Mealy bug, b) spider mite, c) scale, d) aphid, e) white fly,
f) fungus gnat, g) slug, h) "sooty black mold"

by the novice for fungus. This mistaken identity typically sends the horrified plant owner racing out the door to the nearest garden shop for a bottle of fungicide. But make no mistake about it. Take a closer look. This is not smooth-surfaced fungus. This is lumpy, bumpy, fuzzy mealy bugs. Furthermore, this bug (and others) leaves behind a calling card. It excretes a sticky, transparent waste product called honeydew that sticks to your plant's leaves or falls on your wooden floors or carpet. This honeydew just happens to be a favorite medium on which the common and (unlike the harmful fungus you mistook the mealies to be) *harmless* Sooty Black Mold will grow. So add it up: If the strange black stuff is growing on the awful sticky stuff below lumpy, bumpy, fuzzy white ovals, you've got mealy bugs!

Which plants do mealy bugs plague? There's one plant these bugs would sell their mother down the river for. It is the number-one magnet for any and all kinds of insect life—the one and only gardenia. Here, love knows no limit. If you've got ·a gardenia that looks like hell, you can be sure that somewhere in there colonies of mealy bugs with party hats and noisemakers are adding their two cents' worth to the general merriment. After gardenias, mealy bugs will hone in on coleus, jade plants, kalanchoes, *Euphorbias*, some cacti, piggyback plants, *Cyperus*, and hibiscus. In a pinch the following will also do: velvet plant, grape ivy, prayer plants, columneas, Wandering Jews, asparagus ferns, and *Peperomias*. As you can see, a hungry mealy bug is not too discriminating!

Finding this bug is usually very easy because it is white and highly visible. Very often a general perusal of leaves and stems hidden from the light of a plant with sticky honeydew will reveal single bugs or clusters of bugs. In particular, check those all-time favorite breeding and hiding places—the junctures (called nodes) where leaves connect to stems. In cacti and succulents, these hiding places translate to all those tiny crevices and creases on the body of the plant.

What do mealy bugs do to the plants they attack? They insert their mouthpieces (in much the same way a mosquito gets you) into the leaves and stems of a plant. Then they avidly suck its vital juices. While the mouthpiece does its thing, the other end, as you already know, is merrily excreting honeydew.

How do you get rid of mealy bugs? You *don't* follow that popular adage that tells you to spray rubbing alcohol on the plant! What is this about not using alcohol? Why do we say this? The misunderstanding about the use of alcohol to combat mealy bugs is akin to the phenomenon that results from playing the game called Telephone. Here, a phrase is whispered into the ear of the first player, who whispers it to the second player. He tells it to the third, and so on and on down the line. By the twentieth player, the message is already garbled and fuzzy. But by the time it reaches the thirtieth player, it is grossly distorted. By the end of the game, and many interpreting ears later, the final player spins out a series of highly mutated words that carry only fragments of the original message. Everyone has a good laugh and talks about the nature of communication. What is the garbled, mutated, popular misunderstanding about alcohol and mealy bugs? It is that you spray alcohol on the plant with mealy bugs. What is, if you will, the "original message," the correct procedure? You don't spray alcohol, you *put* alcohol *on the mealy bugs* that infest the plant. As you see, some of the original words re-main, but what a difference their mutation makes!

What happens if you go with the popular advice and spray the plant with alcohol? You will burn your plant's tissues, and you will be much the sorrier for it. At this point, an alcohol-spraying customer would cry, "But I already sprayed my plant with alcohol, and nothing bad happened to it." To this we counter, plain and simple: *"You were lucky!* You just happened to spray a tough plant. The gods were in your corner that day. But don't push your luck because luck is all it was." *Alcohol belongs on the back of a mealy bug or on clusters of mealy bugs.* How do you get it there? Take a Q-Tip and dip the fuzzy end in rubbing alcohol. With your fingers, direct this tip to the back of single adult bugs or their colonies. The result is instant death by burning.

But this, unfortunately, is not all there is to it. This "knock 'em out as you find them" technique deals only with the highly visible, stationary adults. But those adults laid eggs. Those eggs hatched or will hatch into not-so-visible, slow-moving, pinkish larvae. The larvae, if al-lowed, will grow up into egg-laying adults. Would you believe, as with most indoor insects, the interval be-tween stages is only seven to ten days! Therefore, to meet the incoming waves of maturing marauders with mouthpieces all set to go, you must continue for at least four weeks going after bugs that made it to adulthood. That way, no new eggs will be laid because you will have destroyed all the adults. Finally, one day, the war will be over. The bugs will be gone. You'll have won!

"But wait a minute!" you're quick to counter with a hysterical note in your voice. "What about larger plants and plants with dense stems, such as a coleus, *loaded* with mealies? Surely you don't expect me to sit down once a week and try to get in there armed only with my little Q-Tip. I'll spend my entire life and still never make a dent!" To this we would say, "Yes. You're absolutely right. The goal is to win without fraying your nerves or having this battle consume your life." Therefore, for severe (and chronic) infestations on dense, multi-stemmed, large plants—where you are hopelessly out-numbered and overpowered—we must escalate the fighting tactic. At this point we want to make something very clear. You don't want to leap into the arena of prepared commercial insecticides as your first line of defense against legions of marauding invaders. Use them only as a *last* resort. Sprays such as the ever-popular and toxic (to practically everything, including you) mal-athion, rotenone, kelthane, and the like, are poisons. That's right, *poisons*. While they will combat the specific bug problem, their misuse can present hazards the average indoor gardener is hardly equipped to handle. So as we prepare to escalate the battle with the mealies (and other insects we'll be getting to), we will cite com-mercial insecticides only as a last solution.

Here is an effective "nontoxic" regime for the densely branched or large plant. With your fingers (or use a tissue if the thought makes your skin crawl) wipe off all bugs you can easily reach without damaging your plant's foliage. Since every mature female carries hundreds of eggs, you're that much more ahead of the game with every bug you get off. Next, if the plant can be carried, take your blighted plant to the sink or shower. Angle the pot so that the rootball doesn't plop out. Now direct a room-temperature jet of water to the undersides of leaves and all crevices. This is where the majority of the bugs reside. Then do a general spray all over the plant. Be sure that the force of the water is strong enough to get in there and knock off the bugs, but it should not be so strong that you unmercifully blast away at the foliage. We want this plant to come away intact instead of looking as though it had been tossed around by a hurricane. It should be as clean of insects as possible, so keep up the shower treatment for a few minutes. While you're at it, now's the time to wipe off that black sooty mold with a soft cloth.

After it's all over, if you dare, take a look at what's collected at the bottom of the sink or tub. You'll be amazed to see how many little white carcasses are on their way down the drain. We guarantee you, it's pure satisfaction. And you've earned it. You can now set your plant down to dry off from this welcomed shower.

Now for the next step. This can also be used alone if your plant is a green giant that can't be toted to the sink or shower. Take any liquid dishwashing detergent and get out your mister. Pour one part liquid detergent to ten parts room-temperature water into the mister and gently shake it up. Next, take your plant and spray this soapy solution all over the foliage. Angle the pot so the solution doesn't get into the soil. Again, pay particular attention to the undersides of leaves and all those other nooks and crannies where mealies love to hide.

An alternate method for small- to medium-sized plants is to mix that same soapy solution in a bucket or the sink. Instead of spraying it on, invert the plant (holding on to the rootball lest it fall in) and swish the foliage around in the soapy water. This technique carries the bonus of thorough coverage. Empty the sink (or whatever) and then fill it with plain water. Invert the plant again to rinse off the soap.

Do this regime, spraying or dunking, once a week for a month. We guarantee that, nine times out of ten, you've seen the last of mealy bugs on that plant.

But for purposes of further edification, let's say that this make-it-up-yourself home remedy doesn't suit you. You hate to mix things. You want something "ready to go." There now exists a fine little preparation on the market for this purpose. It is a small step up in potency from our detergent solution but still keeps you away from any toxic insecticide. It is called Safer Agro-Chem's Insecticidal Soap for Houseplants. Follow the instructions for its use. Note that, unlike our homespun remedy, this product *cannot* be used on palms, jade plants, euphorbias, or delicate ferns. We remind you that you have the option of spraying or dunking small- and medium-sized plants. Spraying has the preparation flying around in the air. Dunking is far more controlled. It is also a lot safer for you. Therefore, with Safer Soap and other more toxic preparations, when possible, opt for the dunking.

Let's say that your mealy bug problem is grave and that you insist upon using a real insecticide. Having been pressed, which one can we recommend? The one to use across the board is malathion. But *read those instrucions carefully* and *believe the precautions!* Where possible, always use the dunk-and-swish technique. And note: You *cannot* use malathion (or any product containing malathion) on any *Crassula* succulent (such as a jade plant) or any of the true ferns, such as a Boston fern. You're okay with an asparagus fern, which isn't a fern at all.

How often do you use it? Remember, we not only have adults to deal with but also maturing larvae on the march and eggs that will hatch to join the legions. Whether you spray or dunk, just as with the other contact preparations, you *must* use the malathion *once a week for a month*. You may be wondering what happens if you do any of these methods just once. The bottom line is that the first time you spray a contact preparation, you hit only those bugs you happen to hit. All the others that your spray doesn't touch are sitting under their little leaf umbrellas waiting for the "funny" rain to cease. Then they can resume their business of chomping away on your plant. Furthermore—and this isn't so cute— that initial spraying will often knock out the weaker and decrepit adults in the population. So the strong, virile ones have a free reign on the territory. One of the husky males meets a similarly husky female. Their offspring are *super* mealy bugs. So don't get lazy and don't feel falsely optimistic. Once you start with any contact preparation, you've got three more applications until you're home free. After that, you should still check the plant occasionally for any signs of a resurgence.

Spider Mites

Let's talk now about the number-two bug most commonly found on houseplants—the spider mite. Spider mites are true eight-legged spiders (insects have six legs). They are very tiny—only one-fiftieth of an inch at maturity. The adults are just barely visible to the naked eye. They come in several different colors (how creative of them). The black, white, and red ones are usually observed on houseplants. Like the true spiders they are, however diminutive, they spin very fine webs, particularly on the undersides of leaves. But once an infestation gets a foothold, those webs will stretch from a

1. Normal growth on foliage plant (Begonia) in proper light (CHAPTER 2).

2. Stretched growth ("eti-olation") on foliage plant due to light deprivation (CHAPTER 2, CHAPTER 8).

3. Plain green plant (*Schefflera venulosa*) for moderate to low light (CHAPTER 2).

4. Variegated plant (*Schefflera venulosa variegata*) for bright light (CHAPTER 2).

5. Plain *Dracaena marginata* for moderate to low light (CHAPTER 2).

6. Highly variegated *Dracaena marginata* 'Tricolor' for very bright light (CHAPTER 2).

7. (*Left*) Slightly overwatered plant
(*Spathiphyllum*) (CHAPTER 3).
8. (*Below*) Drastically overwatered plant
(CHAPTER 3), also suffering from
multiple ills (CHAPTER 1).
9. (*Above*) Practically dead overwatered
plant (CHAPTER 3).

10a. Slight wilt on foliage plant (Chinese evergreen) signals it's time to water.

10b. Recovered plant after watering. (CHAPTER 3).

11. Staked plant (*Dieffenbachia*) long overdue for transplanting (CHAPTER 5).

12. Large plant in dire need of transplant falling out of its small pot (CHAPTER 5).

13. Potbound plant (*Dracaena marginata*) with roots growing out of drainage holes and a network of roots at soil's surface. Both indicate the need to transplant immediately. (CHAPTER 5)

14. Hanging plant (Wandering Jew) desperate for pruning to correct its failing health and straggly appearance (CHAPTER 8).

15. Don't root in water. Don't use sickly cuttings. Don't use cuttings that are too long. (CHAPTER 9)

16. *Ficus* in severe shock, dropping leaves by the minute (CHAPTER 10).

leaf to the stem, then from leaf to leaf and all junctures. Finally they'll show up all over the plant. A closer look into those webs, if you dare, will reveal adults milling about, looking for partners, saying hello to the children, and generally having a ball!

Even though we're talking about a very small bug, once you get the hang of it you'll be able to spot that yellow spider-mite "look" a mile off. It's unmistakable. But if your eyes fail you, use your fingers. If you rub your fingertips back and forth against the upper and under surface of a mited leaf, you will feel the distinctive grainy feeling of webs and mites. So if you're feeling up to it, let your fingers confirm what your eyes suspect.

What plants do these mighty mites prefer? Like any bug that knows a good thing when it sees it, a spider mite would walk over fifty thick-leafed succulents, such as a jade plant, just to take a turn at a gardenia. They also love Scheffleras and palms and ivies. Philodendrons, aluminum plants, and many of the begonias will also do just fine.

What do spider mites do? Like mealy bugs, they suck your plant's precious juices. In so doing, they provide an important clue for detecting their presence: They give those areas on the plant a speckled, mottled, yellow look. This is due to the thousands of punctures by all those mouthpieces, which are enhanced by the yellow death of the cells on the edges of all those holes.

Many plants, even robust, vigorous, healthy ones, often house a mite or two here and there, but on a healthy plant, the tenacious mite never gets so much as a toe in the door in terms of significant population growth. Then the winter months come along. Forgetting that it's time for your plant to rest, you may have continued to water at the frequent intervals you got used to during the active spring and summer months. So now, suddenly, you've overwatered your plant and it is debilitated in its waterlogged state! Then, to prime it for more problems, you actually went and fertilized—out of season—this plant that was already struggling. Now enters the real culprit—the hot dry air created by central heating. And spider mites love hot, dry air! So what happens to those two or three mites aimlessly wandering around on your once-healthy plant? They multiply to create a population explosion. Like any bug, the mites were grateful for the overwatering that debilitated their host. Like any bug, they were also grateful for the ill-advised fertilizing that compounded the plant's problems. But, particularly for spider mites, this dry heat is a godsend. They jump for joy. They leap into action. Spider mite boy meets spider mite girl, and a plant that had only three mites three months ago now has three thousand!

The moral of the story? Spider mites are the most opportunistic and exploitative bugs of all. If you let them get a toe in the door, they'll break the door down!

How do you keep your plants free of this terrible pest? Keep them healthy! What do you do if you suspect or know that a plant in your collection already has mites? First, isolate it! Next, mitigate the effects of that awful dry heat in the winter months by regular, frequent, daily mistings. Twenty times a day isn't too much. This way, you naturally control the spider mite issue.

Do you need to get tougher? Then proceed to the sink or shower treatment described before. When spraying, once again be sure to direct that jet of water to the undersides of leaves and any other area where you suspect bugs to be. Next, move up to that same homemade detergent solution as previously outlined for mealy bugs. Then feel free to continue the escalation to Safer Soap.

If those mites are still hanging in there and you want a commercial insecticide, once again our choice is going to be malathion. Apply it once a week for a month. Be sure to read that label. Be sure to believe those precautions.

Even after the required four-week treatment of malathion, some customers return to declare their plant still has mites. "I can see them. They're there!" We know this person is telling the truth. Mites can get a stranglehold on a favorite breeding ground such as a gardenia or areca palm. Sometimes they lodge there despite all the sprays and all the dunkings in the world. And sometimes, just when you think you've got the problem licked, lo and behold, five weeks later, there are those webs again! Is there anything you can do? Yes. There is one last and usually very effective commercial insecticide that can be resorted to *only as your last line of defense.* This preparation is called a systemic granular insecticide. It is highly toxic and must be used with great care. There are a couple of these systemics currently on the market. But the only one you dare use is the one indicated for houseplants that also says it's okay for tomato plants and other edibles. Rather than attack the bug problem from the outside in, as all of our contact remedies so far have done, this kind of pesticide works the other way—it attacks the problem from the *inside out.* Follow the instructions with extreme care and apply the granules to the surface of the soil right before the next watering is due. At that first watering, X amount of granules will dissolve in a solution, and seep right down into the soil. That solution is absorbed by the roots, pulled up though the stems, and evenly distributed throughout the plant. This systemic insecticide (which will give off that unmistakable bug-spray odor for a few days after its application) will slowly further dissolve with each subsequent watering. For the next eight to twelve weeks the veins all through the plant will be filled with a constant dose of the insecticide.

What happens to the mites sucking juices all over the plant? The moment they stick that mouthpiece in to suck some juice, they ingest the insecticide already in the tissues of the plant. And they die. Sound miraculous? It is, in a way. But remember: These systemics are *real* pesticides. They must not be gaily sprinkled about in a reckless hit-or-miss fashion, as though you were harmlessly salting a batch of french fries. These preparations mean business. When misused, they can be toxic to you!

Scale

Next we turn to scale, the last of the "big three" insects most commonly found on houseplants. Scales are brown and one-eighth-inch long at maturity. While they can be flat, oval, or rounded, the ones you're likely to encounter will be round. They look much like little round turtles stuck on the upper- and undersides of leaves, and up and down the stems and trunks of your plants. By the time they are adult, they are stationary and no longer move about.

Scales should not be mistaken for the sometimes similar-looking brown spore cases borne on the undersides of mature "true ferns," such as a Boston fern (as opposed to an asparagus fern, which isn't a fern at all). This is not to say that a scale will not attach itself to the underside of a fern frond. Indeed, it can and it will. If there's any doubt about which is which, pick off one of the brown spots in question and squeeze it. If it's dry and powdery, you just mashed a spore case containing powder-fine spores. If it squishes under your fingers like any bug, you just killed a scale. To further distinguish the two, like mealy bugs, scales have the unpleasant trait of excreting mold-forming honeydew. That's something no spore could ever do!

Which plants do scales prefer? They're not very choosy, which means they'll take on practically any green target. But they do depart from mealies and mites in that these insects will avidly go after any tough, woody-stemmed plants such as *Ficus* trees, camellias, and hibiscus. Needless to say, the lovely gardenia is always fair game. What parts of these plants do they prefer? Any part! Leaves, stems, trunks, it's all the same.

Where do you look for them? As with mealies, above and around any area on your plant where you see that sticky stuff.

What do these insects do? Like their comrades, mealies and mites, scales suck your plant's juices.

What do you do to get rid of them? Follow the same regime we described earlier for mealies. Just as you were instructed there to wipe off as many bugs as your fingers could reach, take that same tack with scales. Every scale squashed with one hundred eggs that never hatched is one hundred one fewer scales to deal with. If the plant is portable, proceed to the rousing spray in the sink or shower, making a point to direct a jet of water to those areas where the scales are. If the size of the plant precludes the shower treatment, pick up on the step where you spray the homemade soapy detergent solution on the plant. If the plant is small enough, opt for the more effective dunking. Whichever one you do, be sure to do it once a week for a month. If the scales persist, escalate the tactic to the spraying or dunking in the Safer Soap preparation. Be sure to follow through and do it once a week for a month. If a random sampling of brown shells still has live scales squishing under your fingers, escalate the tactic right on up to the real insecticide, malathion. Spray or dunk once a week for a month.

Now, you already know that we're hardly advocates of racing for commercial pesticides to combat bug problems. But we're also realists. For moderate to severe infestations of scales—particularly those occurring on tall, large floor plants such as *Ficus* trees—sometimes the only way out of the woods is to resort to the aforementioned systemic granular insecticide. Why? First, because these tall, large floor plants are the very same plants that scale attacks. Second, because most people do not have ten-foot ladders sitting around the apartment on which to precariously balance, picking off scales one by one. Third, because a ten-foot *Ficus* tree does not easily fit into a sink or tub for a shower. Fourth, because it is not reasonable or realistic to expect to contact spray all the leaves and stems and trunks of such a specimen. Fifth and last, by the time a scale is adult, its shell is more or less impervious to contact sprays. So by all means try the other remedies if you can, but don't feel like a failure when you resort to a systemic to save your scale-ridden green giant.

When you use systemics on other insects, the soft bodies of the offending insects usually decompose and just sort of disappear. But not so with scale. Even though the bug underneath has long since departed from this world, the hard shells tend to hang in there. Therefore, two months after the application of a systemic, don't look at a shell-ridden tree and yell, "The damn stuff didn't work!" They are only shells you're looking at.

Unlike the earlier sampling of shells that you did, the only way to determine in a thorough fashion what's what *now* is to do a systematic regime of random samplings. Pick off a shell here. Take off another from a different section of your tree. Take yet a third one from somewhere else and a fourth one for good measure. Now *squeeze* them. Go on, do it. As you already know, it's the only way to be sure. If the scales under those shells are alive, they will squish. If they're dead, the contents of those shells will be white and powdery. In the ensuing weeks, your continued occasional samplings should find that two out of three, and then three out of three, scales are dead. The squishing will cease.

Well, that takes care of the "top three" offenders on the bug list. Next, we want to touch briefly on some of the lesser insects, those not quite as common on houseplants. But don't think you can sit back and relax through this section. Any and all of these creatures are out there ready to pounce or jump or slide or fly over to your prized plants at any time. They just don't do it quite as often as the big three. What are these insects? They are aphids, white fly, fungus gnats, and slugs. Taken together they're quite a mouthful (perish the thought!)— but not to worry, we'll treat each in turn.

Aphids

First, the aphid, also known as a greenfly and a plant louse. It is pear-shaped, usually wingless, and about one-sixteenth of an inch long when fully grown. It can be in green, brown, black, gray, yellow, or, for good measure, pink.

Where are aphids found? They're found on practically all plants, massing at the tender growing tips, causing new growth to be stunted and deformed. The plants they love begin with the gardenia and continue through to velvet plants, wax plants, coleus, and many of the cacti and succulents.

What do they do? They suck a plant's juices and secrete honeydew.

How do you get rid of them? As the following chapter on pruning a plant for health tells you, one fast way to instantly reduce the population is simply to snip off those very same growing tips that are packed with bugs. Presto, there go one-fourth of the aphids and one-fourth of the bug problem. But, for goodness' sake, don't leave the aphid-infested pieces lying around. With dispatch, get them to the garbage can and close the lid tightly! Next, follow the same regimes suggested all along, but don't resort to commercial sprays here. If you keep after them, you can easily rid your plant of this pesky little bug with strictly nontoxic methods.

White Fly

Next in line: white fly. This white insect is one-sixteenth of an inch long, and can fly. When a plant infested with white flies is jarred or moved, the adults take to flight and scatter, then resettle on the plant (or another one) once the disturbance is over.

Which plants do they prefer? Any plant with soft, juicy leaves. The leaves can be thick and juicy, like an African violet's leaves, or they can be thin and juicy, like those of a coleus or a piggyback plant.

What do they do? They suck juices and make honeydew. The warm summer temperatures will shorten to a mere four or five days the interval between eggs, larvae, adult, and eggs again! So, as you can see, these little bugs can take over in a matter of a few hot days.

What do you do to get rid of them? Fortunately, the flies become relatively inactive in the cool, dark night hours. Therefore, if the little beasts have indeed decided to call your coleus their home, try to *slowly* tiptoe that plant into the bathroom, where you already have the shower going. And quick! Get that foliage under the spray fast, before the bugs have a chance to fly away. Then, follow through with the detergent solution sprays. In addition, sometimes sticky strips of flypaper can be helpful. Give the plant a shake and hope the flies will find the paper!

If you have a real infestation, with clouds of white dots with wings scattering and resettling all day, do not bother resorting to insecticides. Instead, consider throwing the whole business out. In a pinch, those hungry "flying disasters" might take a second look at some of the other plants in your collection. And believe us, this bug defines the word *nuisance*.

Fungus Gnats

Next, to give you a welcome respite from more serious afflictions, let's talk about the very common fungus gnat, a bug for all seasons. First of all, these bugs have nothing to do with fungus. That is, they don't cause it. The "fungus" part of the name derives from the fact that this gnat is attracted to the same conditions that attract fungus—the moist soil found in the pot of a plant that's being overwatered. The common name is through association, not deed.

Fungus gnats are black, almost one-eighteenth of an inch long at maturity, and the adults fly. These minute flies seem to appear out of thin air, and quite often, after a few days, they'll disappear just as mysteriously as they appeared.

What do they do? Nothing terribly harmful. The flying adults are attracted to moist soil that is also fresh and organically rich. There they lay their eggs, which hatch into larvae. All these even smaller larvae do is feed on the dead and decaying matter in the soil. Although you may never have thought about it, this process of decomposition is always going on, one way or another, in a rich potting soil. The larvae mature and then a few days later they fly off. End of problem. As you see, the fungus gnat is a relatively harmless creature, more of an aesthetic nuisance than anything else. It simply borrows your good soil for a few days to perpetuate its species. Therefore, it is rarely necessary to do more about this bug than to shoo it away from the occasional flight near your nose.

The only exception to this "live and let live" attitude may be that rare instance when you have a larvae-endowed pot, with critters milling about in the hundreds. This causes the possessor to wonder, "Is there enough dead and decaying matter to go around? Will all these hungry larvae head for my roots?" If the idea (which is a remote possibility) disturbs you, we offer the following suggestion. Wait until the next time the plant is due for a watering—no sooner! Otherwise you'll compound your plant's problems by overwatering it. (Is it possible that the waterings have indeed been *sooner*, which is what attracted this gnat to your too-moist plant in the first place?) Take the plant to the sink or tub and fill it with room-temperature water so that the water is higher than the rim of the pot. Let the pot sit there for half an hour. You just drowned the juvenile bug population. In the process, your plant got a good soaking. Rarely is a second treatment necessary.

Slugs

Next and last on our list of lesser pests are slugs. These insects range in size from something as relatively reasonable as one-half inch long all the way to a heart-stopping five inches. They come in yellow, brown, black, and shades in between.

While these insects prefer the space of an outdoor garden, the grisly fact is that a slug will often find its way into a greenhouse, where it will slip into the pot of a plant being grown. What kind of a plant does it choose? Never a cactus or succulent! The soil in these plants' pots dries out far too long between waterings to appeal to this moist, dewy little creature. It wants a soil that's as moist and dewy as it is, so it typically slides into the pots of small, leafy plants whose waterings will be frequent and keep the slug happy. The plant, with the slug nicely reposing in some moist little crevice in the soil or a nook in the pot's drainage hole, is shipped to your garden shop. If you forgot to heed the warnings in chapter 1 and in the introduction to this chapter that say inspect plants for bugs before you buy them, you chose this plant and brought it home. Now you have a new plant *and* a new slug.

What do slugs do? They deliver one of life's most unforgettable frights when your fingers unexpectedly come across one! Slugs also chomp away on all parts of a plant—leaves, flowers, stems, roots. By the way, they do this during the dark night hours, so they can retreat to their hiding places for the bright daylight hours. Wherever slugs crawl, they leave behind a glistening trail of slime that dissipates in a few hours. You'll see that slime track on the sides of the pot or stretched in a macabre drape across your plant's leaves. It's not a pleasant thought and hardly a pretty sight. But, looking on the bright side, that telltale slime track is positive proof that you have an uninvited new pet in the house.

What do you do about slugs? Would you believe you pick them off? You don't have to turn off the lights, hide behind the sofa, and a half hour later leap out with a "Ah ha! Got'cha!" But to tell you the truth, the true-life variation isn't too different. Just calm down and be brave. If this "hide in the dark and pick off" routine is more than you can stomach, use the "dunk and drown" procedure previously described for fungus gnat larvae. Again, let the pot sit totally immersed in water for a half hour. Do this and you can rest assured your slimy creature of the night will be no more.

Fungus

Before we leave the land of pests that plague your plants, let's talk briefly about fungus. Fungus is not an insect, it's a plant. We include it in this chapter right along with bugs because it's such a common affliction. When you look for fungus, do not expect the spectacular wooly growth you find on a sixty-day-old slice of bread. Do not expect that jungle of growth that flourishes on wizened, old carrots quietly decomposing at the bottom of your vegetable bin. Fungus on houseplants is not nearly so visually dazzling, but it can be very lethal. It can start innocuously enough in small, soft spots of various colors—white, gray, yellow, brown, black—on the leaves of your plants. If left untreated, the spots will increase in size. Then they will form *large* soft splotches. The affected areas may also be stems or flowers or all three!

What does the fungus (mold, blight, rot) do? With the exception of the harmless sooty black mold that you've already met more times than you want to think about, a fungus insidiously invades the tissues of a plant and destroys them. If its course runs unchecked, it will destroy its host—your plant.

What causes fungus? Where does it come from? Fungus is produced and spread through powder-fine, airborne reproductive bodies called spores. Spores float through the air and alight here and there at random. If a spore happens upon a suitable medium (such as your plant's leaves or stems) and conditions are right, it starts to grow. If conditions stay right, it starts to spread.

What constitutes the right conditions? Some plants are born susceptible to fungus. These are all the begonias, particularly the sensitive Rex variety. Also susceptible are gloxinias and that friendly little plant, the African violet. And even the common geranium will willingly play host to a fungus invasion. But make no mistake about it: The waterlogged, water-saturated, waterdamaged leaves and stems of *any* plant resulting from overwatering will also create the right conditions. Spores need water—excessive water—to do their thing. They rarely do it alone. They need your help and cooperation.

What measures can you take to prevent fungus? First, be aware of the highly susceptible plants in your collection. Remember that water is the agent that is critical to the happiness and well-being of fungus, and do not spray-mist plants prone to fungus. This doesn't mean you should frantically get the hair dryer to blow-dry the leaves of a Rex begonia that you accidentally misted. It means you shouldn't go out of your way to mist these leaves.

Second, for heaven's sake, don't overwater your plants! As chapter 3 on watering plants tells you, an overwatered plant is nothing less than a "sick sitting duck" all primed for the inevitable fungus onslaught.

Third, don't overcrowd plants. Fungus loves still air, particularly if there's a cold chill to it. It doesn't like freely circulating air of any temperature.

What can you do if fungus blight has already struck? You don't have to sit there helpless; there are measures you can take to reverse the blight. The first measure, as the following chapter on pruning stresses, is to *cut off the affected areas immediately!* That's right. Cut them off and carry the spore-laden pieces to the trash receptacle. Place them inside and seal the lid tightly. Next, feel free to use commercial fungicides, such as Zineb, Ferbam, and Benamyl. Follow the instructions carefully, and be sure to see the regime through to the last application.

Now . . . a few parting words on the general subject of bugs and disease. There comes a time with many things in life, including plants, when you're truly outnumbered. The wonderful joys of indoor plant culture are fading. The bugs are too many. The blight is too great. The fear of contagion is too real. The plant is hopelessly suffering and so are you. This is the time, my friends, when you should look a bad situation squarely in the eye. Remember that plants are to be enjoyed for the immense pleasure they can give. Summon your courage. With the most positive resolve, throw the plant and the whole mess out. And call it a day!

8.

How <u>Not</u> to Wallow in the "I Can't Bear to Prune My Plants" Syndrome

Let us ask you something: Have you ever gotten your hair cut? Have you ever filed your fingernails? And, if we can get personal for a moment, have you ever trimmed your toenails? Unless you are not of this earth, your answers have got to be a unanimous "yes, yes, and yes," maybe followed by, "Why, hundreds, *thousands* of times! Everybody does these things. It's natural. It's normal. What absurd questions!"

"Absurd," you say? Then while you're still laughing, maybe you can tell us this: *Why is it that you refuse to prune your plants?* "But it's not the same thing!" is the typical response. "Pruning is unnatural. It's artificial. I just let my plants grow the way they want to, the way they were intended to. Besides (and here's where things get emotional), I can't bear to prune my plants!"

Well, finally we get down to the truth—most of you truly can't bear to even think of touching your precious greenery. But the rest of your typical answer is loaded with untruths, such as pruning is unnatural or artificial. Nothing could be further from the truth. To *not* prune is the unnatural act. How can we possibly suggest such a thing? Very easily. Plants growing wild in their natural habitat don't just merrily grow on and on in an uninterrupted sequence that extends the length of their lives. Hardly! Nature has all sorts of ways to cut off, cut back, lop off, dice off, to one way or another prune back portions of her plants growing in jungles.

Still not convinced? Then let's look at one small "slice" (you'll pardon the choice of words) of a tropical jungle to see if we can't find some examples for you. We don't need to have elephants rampaging about to set the mood. A few monkeys swinging around in the treetops should do it. And let's throw in a dozen colorful birds. These wonderful creatures and hundreds of other species not as visible are quietly or noisily going about their business amid, behind, under, among, on top of, and in some cases *in* the bounty of plants sharing this same place on earth. Now sitting somewhere on the jungle floor in filtered sun is a three-foot *Dracaena* plant just like yours in the dining room. Only this one doesn't live in a pot. Instead of the family kitty for company, it has lions and tigers that roar and crouch down and jump out from under the cover of its leaves.

Let's take this "wild" *Dracaena* and see what happens to it. Remember the monkeys happily swinging around in the trees? Well, one of them has left his play in the high altitudes to seek the jungle floor, where he is busily foraging for fallen nuts. As he pauses to retrieve a nut that has fallen into a rock crevice, guess what he happens to grab onto for support? None other than the little *Dracaena!* That monkey's got the top of the trunk in his fist. As he bends over, guess what happens next? His grip tightens. That, coupled with the lurching of his body, suddenly snaps off the top of the *Dracaena*. If it's the monkey you're rooting for, not to worry! He got the elusive nut. And, without so much as a backward glance, he's already ambling down the jungle lane throwing out the shell in his wake. He's okay.

But what about the plant? The majority of you "I can't bear to prune my plants" folks probably think, "Well, the plant's *not* okay. What a miserable story." The fact is the plant *is* okay, and this is not a miserable story. This is the natural way of things, the natural order. Because the story doesn't end here. That three-foot *Dracaena*, suddenly reduced to two feet, doesn't turn into petrified wood and sit there cemented in its new size and shape for the rest of its days. It *does* something, something that Nature programmed it and the millions of plants like it to do to ensure the continuation of its growth and the perpetuation of its species despite thoughtless monkeys and all the vicissitudes of rough, tough jungle life.

What does it do? *It branches out.* Right below where its growing tip was so rudely yanked off will grow at least one, possibly two, or maybe even three new trunks that will take over and carry on the tradition of growth inching toward the heavens. If all these new trunks weren't compensation enough for being mugged by a monkey, the *Dracaena* may well experience the bonus of additional branching. This branching can occur anywhere along its trunk from the point where it broke all the way down to the soil line, thereby transforming its single lonesome trunk into a lush, multitrunked beauty. Is this the plant you're crying over? Dry those tears. If it had been a contest, the monkey got the short end of this stick!

This is only one of the hundreds of stories of natural

pruning occurring in our little slice of the jungle. For instance, not ten feet away from the *Dracaena* is a variety of creeping fig (*Ficus pumila*), much like yours at home, that has created a lovely, soft, green carpet on the jungle floor. But along comes a hungry tortoise. What does he spy? That very same green carpet, which to him is like your coming upon a bin of fresh romaine lettuce. What does he do? He helps himself to the banquet, munching away until his stomach can hold no more. Once satiated, he ambles away even more slowly than he arrived. Now is this "it" for the hole that the turtle ate in the carpet? No, not at all. Not only will the plant grow back, but it will fill in fuller and lusher than ever before. Everywhere that turtle bit off growing tips, the stems behind the bite will eventually send out multitudinous new stems that otherwise would not have grown.

Are there more tales of natural pruning to tell? You bet. There are as many tales as there are plants and animals and forces of Nature all interacting with one another. There is the once-scrawny, now-lush Schefflera that says thank you to the overanxious bird who came in too fast for a landing and broke off the plant's growing tip. There is the yucca that has never looked better, that says thank you to the nervous giraffe who backed into it one morning and broke it in half. There's the *Cordyline* that says thank you to the mold that rotted out its old growing tip and now basks in multitrunked splendor. There is the climbing philodendron that was afraid its growing tips would never take the beating of a wild tropical storm. Fortunately they didn't withstand the high winds but snapped off. Now that plant's growth is more beautiful. In the future, the plant won't be afraid of the fury that has become its friend.

The moral of the story? Over and over again in the

natural world we have examples of plants not only sur-
viving but in fact grateful to the agents of their natural
pruning. Had they not been in the right place at the
right time for this intervention, none of these plants
would have fulfilled its shapely destiny. What's the message for you nonpruners out there? Put away your misplaced sentiment and fears born of ignorance. Remember
how good you felt and how good your hair looked the
last time you got those split ends trimmed off? Then,
once and for all, put aside any lingering pockets of resistance and look at the overwhelming facts. Pruning
doesn't hurt or hinder your plants' growth, it *helps*. It
is as much in sync with the natural order of things as
the forces within a seed that want to make a plant.

Let's learn the why's and when's and how to's of
pruning. Why do we prune plants? We prune for three
reasons: One, for beauty and to ensure that a plant
realizes its true potential. Two, for health and to treat
those ills that can be remedied by pruning. Three, to
obtain cuttings for the purpose of propagation.

Let's start with beauty, with aesthetics, with how things
look. Pruning for beauty is divided into two techniques.
The first is more *groom* than prune; therefore, we call it
grooming. It applies to all plants; that is, it covers the
vast majority of plants capable of branching (such as
Swedish ivies, geraniums, Wandering Jews, all the *Dracaenas*, all the *Pileas*, almost all of the philodendrons,
almost all of the *Peperomias*, all the *Ficus* trees, and thousands of others). Grooming also applies to those plants,
very much in the minority, that are not capable of
branching because their leaves emanate from a central
growing point, or "crown." (These plants include Af-

rican violets, ferns, spider plants, gloxinias, and so forth.) The second technique is pruning to promote growth where you want it. This technique benefits only plants capable of branching.

Grooming improves on what Mother Nature's aesthetics would tolerate and let be. For example, in or out of the jungle, sometimes even the most beautiful plant will produce a few yellow leaves or a dead branch. As you already know, this is normal attrition and is part of the natural scheme of things. But is it your habit to let these yellow leaves ripen on the vine before you remove them? Do you delay cutting off your tree's dead branch until the wild cavorting of your ninety-pound Great Dane does the job for you? Furthermore, do you wait for your African violet's spent flowers to curl up into little wizened balls before you're pressed into action? Is the look of bent, broken leaves on a spider plant that took a tumble okay with you? Are you waiting for the cat to reform herself before you intercede on behalf of the shredded leaves of your palm tree? We hope not! *Act with dispatch.* Remove any offending part that spoils the perfection of an otherwise beautiful plant. This grooming isn't trying to "fool Mother Nature." It's helping her along! What else does it do? In the same instant that grooming improves and restores your plant's beauty, it makes you feel better too!

Let's look at the second technique that is only for plants capable of branching—pruning to promote growth where you want it. We'll focus on the following five words that say it all: *Big is not necessarily better.* What does this mean? It means that, unless your decor insists upon an exclusionary straight-up-and-down look, your single-stemmed rubber tree that has finally hit the ceiling may well be no more cause for celebration than the lady who has grown her hair down to her knees. Why not? Your tree, through your failure over the years to prune to induce branching, has been judiciously denied the opportunity to act out the full message of its genetic code. The fortunate fact is that the average rubber tree— and many other plants capable of lateral growth—may well go ahead and occasionally branch out all by itself, but just imagine how this same rubber tree would look if your pruning shears had intervened all through the years. Today, that single-stemmed, ten-foot broomstick would be a multitrunked rubber tree sporting numerous arching branches loaded with thick, glossy, green leaves. It would be a real prize plant, a tree to be proud of!

Similarly, consider that other favorite, the Wandering Jew (*Zebrina pendula*). Unfortunately, because of the public's fear and ignorance of pruning, once this plant leaves the greenhouse where it was grown, it will rarely feel the touch of a human hand again! If you have a Wandering Jew growing in your window, it's probably hanging down a good three feet, right? Instead of a gloriously lush, compact, branching plant with leaves all over, look at what you've got. Like the lady with the long hair, you've got length all right. But in the single-minded pursuit of length, you've got a plant that looks as though someone with a perverse sense of humor glued a few pieces of long brown string to a pot, flipped them so they'd dangle straight down, pasted on a leaf here and a leaf there, and then—in the sustained spirit of humor that mimicks true life—way, way, *way* down at the ends of the strings, our jokester attached little clusters of leaves. Do you consider this maze of brown strings ending in green pom-poms a vision of loveliness? Is this a plant you're proud of? Nonsense! Like a lot of other things in life, with plants there is no automatic glory in sheer length or height! This Wandering Jew that invites ridicule is a pathetic, neglected mess. It and millions like it could have and should have been pruned. (See photograph 14.)

Of course, in cutting back, height or length is sacrificed, but only momentarily. In time the pruned rubber tree will hit the ceiling just as surely as its hell-bent-on-height counterpart. In time the trimmed-as-you-go Wandering Jew will reach the desired three-foot length. And they won't do it looking like telephone poles or plucked chickens. These plants will be full-feathered peacocks!

Now let's talk about pruning for health. What kind of pruning is this? It's a method applicable to both crowning and branching plants that tries to prevent problems before they strike, and it's sometimes part of the cure *after* the fact of trouble. Take the case of fungus attack. Some plants, such as African violets and begonias, are *born* susceptible to this blight. Their tissues always look inviting to the seeds or spores of fungus that float invisibly through the air. But you're not out of the woods if your collection doesn't include one of these fungus-favorite plants. This blight will indiscriminately attack any plant whose tissues have been damaged or undermined due to overwatering, chilling, bruising, or disease. In a pinch, fungus will also seek out decomposing old leaves that are due to normal attrition on an otherwise perfectly healthy plant. And once it gets a foothold, it can spread and make life miserable for all parts of your plant. Want to go the easy route of prevention? Then prune off dying leaves and any damaged foliage before the spores find them! Is it too late? Are you already eyeballing a full-blown case of white (or black) powdery splotches on your plant's leaves? Then resort to three lines of defense: First, isolate the plant. Second, treat it with a fungicide. Third, go for immediate results: *Prune off* those leaves most severely affected, thereby immediately getting off the worst areas of blight.

What other ills can pruning prevent or help cure? Insects such as fungus gnats love a plant that's been "let go to pot" in a tangle of decomposing old leaves competing with healthy leaves. These insects jump for joy at a nice collection of fallen, rotting leaves on the soil's surface. These bugs are no fools. They know a good thing when they see it, and they hide in, play in, feed on, and breed amid the bounty of decaying plant tissues, courtesy of your neglect. Want to prevent these bug problems before they strike? Then don't play right into the hands of these opportunistic insects—prune off dying leaves when they start to die. Pick up leaves from the soil's surface before they start to accumulate.

What do you do if fungus gnats are already calling your plant home? Isolate the plant, treat it with the methods outlined in the preceding chapter, and prune off and clean up the play and breeding grounds!

Pruning won't prevent an attack of those other common houseplant bugs, such as spider mites, scales, mealy bugs, and aphids, but it can be an immense help after an invasion. How so? After you isolate the plant once again, and take the appropriate remedies, you have the option of pruning off the sections of the plant most severely infested. This pruning literally cuts out large segments of the bug population and instantly puts you way ahead of the game.

What other conditions does pruning remedy? In our chapter on overwatering we mention the life-threatening wilt that a badly root-rotted plant will succumb to when the plant doesn't have enough live roots left to supply water to its remaining leaves. Only one last-chance procedure will give this plant a shot at survival—pruning back the plant's foliage to reduce the burden on the failing root system. Does it work? Without the pruning, the plant hasn't a prayer!

Does pruning affect other cures? In our chapter on transplanting we talk about the wisdom of taking a few minutes to examine the condition of a plant's rootball before proceeding to place it in the new larger pot. This pause enables you to make sure the visible roots are healthy and in working order. If you spy any soft black areas that spell rot in that rootball, what should you do? Prune them off! Get rid of them. If you are compelled to shave off a portion bigger than one-fourth of the roots, you must compensate the plant for this loss by cutting back one-fourth of its foliage on top, thereby maintaining that ratio critical to all plants of so many roots to so many leaves.

Pruning will also remedy "stretch" growth (called etiolation) exhibited by any plant grown in far less than the preferred light. (See photographs 1 and 2.) This condition (gravely aggravated by overwatering) explains, for instance, that sudden burst of weak, pale, flimsy growth produced by Scheffleras, coleus, Swedish ivies, and myriad other plants, including cacti and succulents, being grown in less light than they need. Sometimes the deterioration can be a sad sight indeed. It is analogous to your sitting at the bottom of a very tall, dark box, desperately craning and stretching your neck to its fullest extent in a futile effort to get to some light.This is exactly what your light-starved plant is doing in its eternal optimism, hoping that further up there exists the necessary light. The point is that this weak, low-light-induced growth must be pruned right back to that point on the stem(s) where the deprivation began. (And for goodness' sake, get that plant into some decent light.) This phenomenon also explains "The Mystery of the Incredible Shrinking Trunk." A *Dracaena marginata* arrives at your home with a nice, thick, robust three-inch-diameter trunk. Over the years not only does the trunk *not* increase in diameter but in fact it shrinks! It goes from three inches to two inches, and now it's pencil-thin, barely able to support the weight of the foliage at its head. Prune that plant right back to the point where the trunk started to thin out. New trunks will sprout right below the cut. (And, once again, get that plant into some good light!)

Finally, we come to pruning for purposes of propagation. This is the pruning you do to cut off pieces of one plant in order to make a new plant. For example, to make a new Swedish ivy, you cut off terminal tip cuttings from an old Swedish ivy. To make a new African violet, you cut off a leaf from an old African violet. To make a new spider plant, you cut off a runner from an old spider plant. To make a new snake plant, you cut off a sucker from an old snake plant. To make two new asparagus ferns, you cut the old plant in half. (These methods and more, plus what to do with cuttings, will be treated in the following chapter on propagation.)

You may have noticed the occasional overlapping of the three categories of pruning—for beauty, for health, and for propagation. That is, the same snip for health that removes an old decaying yellow leaf also instantly improves a plant's beauty. The snip on top to take off a terminal cutting to make a new plant triggers welcomed branching to the lucky plant under that cut. While you appreciate the merits of one-snip-for-two desirable results, let's move on to when to prune your plants.

Basically, it breaks down like this: If you're pruning for health, do it *when and as the need arises*. That is, if fungus attacks your chilled begonia on December 1, your remedy pruning starts December 1. If it's preventative pruning for health or grooming for beauty, do it *when and as the need arises*. That is, snip faded blossoms off your African violet when and as they fade, and snip the yellow leaves off your Swedish ivy when and as they yellow.

All pruning for propagation and *all* pruning for branching plants *to promote growth where you want it* is very much a seasonal matter. How so? As you already know, your plants are dormant during the winter months. To take any kind of cutting for propagation off a sleeping plant is courting failure because that cutting is every bit as asleep as its parent. When *do* you prune for cuttings to make new plants? In the active-growth spring and summer months (March through October), when the cutting will share its parent's get-up-and-grow spirit and will want to hurry up and root. This is the same season to do pruning to promote growth where you want it on plants capable of branching—to induce *more* branching. This pruning ideally starts in February or March and continues throughout the growing season.

Now that you know why and when to prune, it's time to find out *how* to prune plants. To make it easy for you, first we're going to show you the simple, very limited techniques for the relatively small percentage of plants whose foliage grows out of a central crown. Then we'll treat the broader techniques for the majority of plants that branch.

As you may recall, the foliage of plants such as African violets, spider plants, and ferns basically grows one way— out of a central crown. These plants don't have trunks whose growing tips can be manipulated to make more trunks, and they don't have branches whose growing tips can be manipulated to make more branches.

How do you prune such plants? Let's let a typical year in the life of an average African violet show you the events that will dictate the pruning technique. The date is January 1. You had a New Year's Eve party, and you're about the business of setting your apartment straight again. As you bend down to retrieve an overflowing ashtray, you accidentally back into your African violet sitting on the windowsill. What's the damage report? Two leaves are bent and broken. There's no recourse but to cut them off. How do you do it? Look at your plant. Do you see how a stem connects the damaged leaf to the plant? Make your cut with a pruning shears or with any sharp household scissors right where the stem attaches to the plant, thereby cutting off the leaf and stem in one snip. Lest there be any misunderstanding, snipping off just the leaf is not enough. This is biting off the "lolly" but leaving the "pop" behind. To do it right, you must snip off the stem too because a headless stem left on a plant is going to slowly die and eventually fall off, all the while flashing an invitation to fungus to "come and get me." You already know that you don't play around with fungus, particularly where African violets are concerned. Pay attention to details and locate your snips where they count!

Two months have passed. It's now March. Very much in step with the advent of spring and encouraged by your fertilizing, your violet is sending out new leaves from its crown and is already in bloom. Now and once a week throughout the growing season (March through October) you check for flowers on their way out, and you snip them off accordingly.

It's April. Your violet is looking so splendid that you decide you must take a leaf off it to make another plant. You follow the same exact procedure set down to prune off January's casualty leaves, but this time, as with any cutting destined to make a new plant, you make sure to choose a flawless, perfect leaf with which to start a second generation of violets.

It's June. Things are humming along. The leaf cutting "took" perfectly and is already making a new little African violet. But then one day your weekly inspection reveals what looks like clusters of white cotton on one of your plant's leaves. A closer look tells you that that "cotton" is mealy bugs. You follow the remedies for getting rid of this pest as outlined in the previous chapter, and you also opt for pruning off the leaf that is the hot-bed of the infestation. You follow the standard procedure for cutting off leaves.

Now the month is November. Your violet is dormant, it's sleeping out the winter. There's no need to groom off spent flowers weekly because your plant ceased blooming several weeks ago and won't start up again until February or March. You use waterings as the time to check your plant's foliage to make sure all's well. In the process of a watering you notice that a lower, older leaf is starting to yellow. You prune it off. Another watering uncovers some white "powder" on a few leaves. That "powder" is fungus. As part of the treatment, you snip off the leaves most blighted.

It's the night of December 31. In one hour the doorbell will start ringing and your house will fill up with revelers ready to bring in the new year with style. In a flash you remember the toll last year's party cleanup took on your plant. Just to be on the safe side, you place your perfectly groomed, robustly healthy, gorgeous African violet on top of the tallest bookcase you have.

Let's look at the more varied pruning techniques for plants that do have regular stems or trunks or branches that can be induced to make *more* stems or trunks or branches. These are branching plants. Their numbers monopolize most of the plant world, and they include many popular houseplants such as Swedish ivies, all the *Dracaenas*, many of the philodendrons, many of the *Peperomias*, all of the *Pileas*, all of the *Ficus* trees, and hundreds of others. The branching mechanism of these plants lets you do more than just prune off a yellow leaf here or a faded flower there. With these plants you can also prune to promote growth where you want it! Let's let the events of a typical year in the life of an average Swedish ivy show you how to do it.

It's late January. Your Swedish ivy is still fast asleep, but in a matter of weeks, the growing tips at the very end of every stem are going to wake up. Left to their own devices, these stem tips will start to increase in length, which is how the plant grows. Therefore, right now, before they wake up, you must do something to these growing tips to promote the desired results—

branching! *What* do you do to the growing tips to get them to branch? You cut them off! *Why* do you cut them off? Contained in the growing (or terminal) tips of every stem are auxins (hormones) that inhibit branching further down on the stem. When you cut off the growing tip (or more), you remove these hormones, thereby permitting lateral branching to commence directly below that cut on the stem, and potentially anywhere else from that point on down to the soil line.

How do you do it? You can pinch off the growing tips of stems with your fingernails, or you can snip them off with pruning shears or any sharp scissors. Exactly *where* on the stem do you pinch or snip? Right above a "node." A node is that juncture where a leaf (or branch) is or used to be attached to a stem. (The space between nodes is called the internode.) A cut right above a node won't leave that awful looking bare stump that will slowly decompose and eventually fall off. Pruning cleanly above a node maintains your plant's appearance *and* health. How much do you cut off? Because your foot-long plant is already nicely branched and shapely, there's no reason to snip or pinch off any more than, say, a one-inch section from the tip of every stem. This snip gets rid of the hormones, thereby ensuring the continued branching out of this plant, but doesn't trim back any more of the stem than is necessary. (If, however, that one-foot Swedish ivy under those terminal tips is a real mess— if its growth is rangy, lopsided, messy, and out of control—you would do much more pruning to bring it back into bounds. In this case, you would cut all the stems back a good six inches, thereby cutting back half the plant's length. The dictum is, the worse the plant looks, the more you have to prune back.)

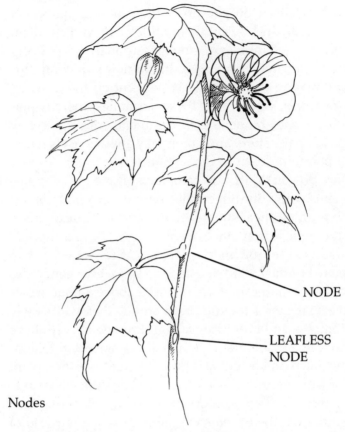

NODE

LEAFLESS
NODE

Nodes

Having done your "early bird" pruning to get your
Swedish ivy off and running on the right foot, the idea
is to continue pinching or snipping off growing tips *once
a month* throughout the spring and summer months
(March through October).

It's April. You are so thrilled at how beautiful your
plant has become that you want to try your hand at
propagation. How do you do it? You prune a couple of
five-inch-long sections from the ends of stems in perfect
condition. (On this plant you don't have to look too far

to find stems like this!) These sections are appropriately called stem cuttings and are the number-one method of propagation for branching plants. (Check the following chapter on propagation about how to root these cuttings.) By the way, what happens to the stems that sacrificed five inches of their length to perpetuate their species? Once again, they're reimbursed by the guaranteed branching below the snip.

It's July. Your plant is feeling a bit peaked in the intense heat. It indicates this discomfort with the yellowing of a few leaves. What do you do? You prune them off, making sure your snips take off the stems (petioles) that attach these leaves to the branch.

It's the first week in September. You do the last pinch or snip to growing tips to induce the final round of branching because soon your Swedish ivy will slow its rate of growth as it gets ready to rest for the long months of winter.

It's the first week of December. Your plant is fast asleep, but that's okay with you. It's taking a well-deserved rest. As the snow starts to accumulate on the ground outdoors, inside your Swedish ivy reposes in resplendent beauty. It's full, it's compact, it's a joy to behold.

Let us leave you with one final word about pruning, and that is the matter of good housekeeping. If a little film of dust is collecting on some of your plants' leaves, get rid of it! (Use a dampened soft cloth—nothing else.) If a household spider sets up house among your precious greenery, send it packing! Let nothing and no one interfere with the shimmering beauty you helped to create.

Now you know the tools, the techniques, the tricks of the pruning trade. You'll never walk into another plant shop like ours and utter at the sight of all that luscious greenery, "How *do* they do it?" Now you know. It's all in the timely trim. It's all in the pinch. Go to it!

9.

How <u>Not</u> to Have the Maternity Ward Resemble a Mortuary

or The Joys of Propagation

Propagation: The process of making new plants from old plants. Cutting: A piece of a plant used to grow a whole new plant. Failure: The opposite of success. Too much of this can be . . . Discouraging: The feeling of not wanting to try again.

Having defined our terms, are you one of the millions of plant enthusiasts whose enthusiasm for propagation stalls at the feared "cut" part of the word "cutting"? Or, has your enthusiasm for propagation plummeted to zero because all those "little ones" made from "big ones" turned into dead ones, and you just don't have the heart to try again?

Well, buck up! If your problem is resistance to and fear of cutting a piece off your plant in the first place, stop right now and flip back to chapter 8 on pruning. This chapter opens with a slice of jungle life in the raw. It has monkeys breaking off the tops of plants; it has giraffes backing into trees, snapping them in half; it has birds crash-landing on and breaking off the tips of trees. It has everything but herds of elephants trampling

151

everything in sight to show you how perfectly natural and how perfectly necessary these acts of pruning are to the plants so blessed. This outside intervention interrupts (and how!) the growth pattern of these jungle plants. But not to worry, the plants are compensated twofold. First, the breakage triggers lush branching that otherwise might not have occurred. Second, when a giraffe's rear end backs into a tree, the impact sends pieces of that plant literally flying through the air. Some of these pieces will root to perpetuate the species. These pieces are called cuttings.

If the source of your deflated enthusiasm for propagation is not the taking of cuttings but rather what happens to them *afterwards*, take heart! There is no great mystery to this business of making new plants from old plants. All you have to know is how to do it! To get you off on the right foot, we're going to tell you, in the order they most frequently occur, the three big don'ts of propagation: *where not* to root a cutting, *when not* to root a cutting, and *which cutting* to avoid in the first place. After you've absorbed this general information that applies to all cuttings, we'll show you seven of the easiest and most popular ways of making new plants from old plants.

If you think pruning is satisfying, if you think fertilizing is productive, the real rewards of indoor gardening yet await you. Propagation that works does it all!

What's the first "don't" of propagation? *Don't root in water!* How's that?" you cry. "But I've always rooted in water! My mother (the expert) roots her cuttings in water. All my plant books and all the information I've ever gotten says to root in water!" Yes, that's why 50 percent of your cuttings never made it and why most of your mother's cuttings never made it either. Any plant book or other source of advice that says root in water is wrong. *Wrong!* Why? Think about it. Nature does not intend that her landlocked plants be rooted in something as contrary to soil as water. Do you recall the *Dracaena* that had its head pruned off by the monkey in chapter 8? You may also recall that the broken piece did not cascade down into a bucket of water left by a passing native, nor did the piece tumble through the jungle for a five-mile roll to the nearest lake. No! The instant the monkey loosened his grip on the trunk, that one-foot piece of *Dracaena* fell down on nothing other than ground, soil, the good earth. There it stayed, and there it eventually rooted.

Is it possible you're still not convinced? Then let's recall exactly what happened to the last batch of cuttings you rooted in water. You start out with five cuttings. Right off the bat, four rot out and die. Four cuttings subtracted from five cuttings leaves one cutting. Since you're no stranger to this kind of failure, you're still grateful—one cutting is 100 percent more than *no* cutting. Days turn into weeks. From time to time you add fresh water to the jar. Even so, green slime forms on its sides, the water is murky, and there's that too-earthy smell that reminds you of the air over the puddle at the bottom of a defunct old well. Just when you think you can't live one minute longer with this thing that looks and smells like a neglected fish tank, you're reprieved! The cutting has made roots. The day has finally come to trade in (and throw away) the messy jar and water for a pot and soil. But getting this cutting into a pot is no easy task. You worry (and rightly so) about breaking all those fragile roots suddenly exposed to the air. You try desperately to arrange them—without destroying half—so they'll all get their fair share of soil. Then with trembling hands you give the soil a drink of water and walk away, not entirely thrilled or optimistic about the procedure. Experience has taught you to be prepared the next morning for the inevitable sight of this cutting flopped over the pot like a piece of lettuce that didn't find its way back to the refrigerator. While the thoughts race—"What's wrong? What happened? Why didn't it work?"—your cutting quietly folds up and dies.

Do you need more convincing? Does this dismal mortality rate not impress you? Then let's explain why this rooting-in-water business almost always fails sooner or later. Let's start with the "sooner." Do you know why four out of five cuttings "kicked the bucket"—or was it the jar?—right at the outset? The answer is these cuttings did not come off water lilies; these cuttings came from land plants whose stem tissues are designed to tolerate the quantity and frequency of water produced by normal rainfalls. These stems are *not* designed to withstand a twenty-four-hour-a-day immersion in water, so they rot!

Then again, as with other things in Nature, there's the exception to the rule. In this case the exception is the one stem in five that does not rot. This stem survives and goes on to produce roots. But then, the problem becomes the condition of these same roots. How so? Roots that emerge from a cutting trapped in a jar of water cannot will themselves out of that jar. Since they can't change their environment, they change themselves. They modify their cellular structure in order not to rot and in order to extract life-sustaining oxygen not from the soil but from water.

So here we have roots that are to be congratulated because they bucked big odds to bridge the gap from land to water. But these roots are not going to live in water forever. Even though they've forgotten it, *you* know these roots belong to a land plant. With the passage of time the day eventually comes when they must get out of the water and, with your help, into some soil in a pot. This brings us to the "later" part of the sooner-or-later failure factor of rooting in water. The sad irony in all this switching back and forth business is this: To the degree that these roots successfully adapted to water, they now will experience that same degree of difficulty in readjusting to the land. In essence what we have here is a creature born with lungs who belongs on land but who gets snatched off the land and thrown in the drink. Once there, it flounders around but manages to make the changes. It turns its lungs into gills, but just as it's getting the hang of breathing oxygen from water, you net it and tell it that it's time to turn those gills back into lungs and return to the land. The problem is that this time the schizophrenic roots can't make the switchover fast enough. The soil you so painstakingly placed around these roots is foreign to them. Even with a watering, the amount of water this soil holds no more helps these distressed, gasping roots than a fish on a dry dock is helped by being sprinkled with water. The cutting wilts, then it dies.

What does all this talk—of plants and lungs and fish and gills and the trouble that results when you try to mix them—tell you? It says that no matter what you read, no matter what you hear, no matter what even your mother says—*don't root your cuttings in water!*

If some morning you should head for the front door in a heated rush and accidentally break off a piece of a foliage plant, in this instance, yes, you can quickly plunk this unexpected cutting in a glass of water. But only as a temporary stopgap measure.

An excellent rooting medium for all cuttings is one or

a combination of the following: sand, perlite, vermiculite, or peat moss. If you think you like sand (or if experience has already so indicated), go ahead and use it, or try vermiculite. If you want to get fancy about it, use a few in combination, such as the mixture of one part sand to one part peat moss, or one part sand to one part vermiculite. You can even be adventurous and use all four in any combination. But if simplicity appeals to you—plus real convenience with guaranteed great results—let us share our formula for a wonderful rooting medium. It reads like this:

1 part soil
1 part peat moss
1 part sand or perlite or vermiculite (or any combination)

Now we ask you, does this formula look familiar? Have you seen this three-part combination before? You bet you have! It is exactly the same as The Village Green Formula for a Great Potting Mixture as described in chapter 4! The good news is that this simple, convenient, easy-to-mix potting soil that is wonderful for your plants is also wonderful for your cuttings, and it guarantees great results! Guess what? It also eliminates the fuss and bother and hazard of having to move your rooted cuttings out of one of the standard rooting mediums and into an "adult" potting soil. Your cuttings are already there! They will continue to grow in the same soil in which they grew their roots! What could be easier? What could be more perfect? This is the rooting medium we use at The Village Green, it is the medium most of our customers use, and now it's yours.

What's the second "don't" of propagation? *Don't take your cuttings during the winter months!* Why not? For the same reasons that you don't transplant or fertilize out of season—because houseplants are asleep, dormant, resting. Therefore, a cutting taken during the inactive winter months (November, December, January) is going to be just as sleepy as its parent. It will sit there like a wooden matchstick stuck in a pot, inactive. It will do absolutely nothing, being just "alive" enough to die. So don't do it! Take your cuttings during the spring and summer months (March through October), ideally in the early months (March to June) when your plants are active and jumping! This is the time of year when the sun's intensity is stronger, the daylight hours are longer, and the nights are shorter. All this coincides with your plant's internal calendar that says it's time to do some real growing. That same message, not coincidentally, is imprinted in the cells of cuttings, so your success rate soars!

What is the third and last "don't" of propagation? *Don't take an inferior cutting if you're seriously interested in multiplying your plants!* For goodness' sake, don't use diseased, bug-infested, blighted, or otherwise inferior pieces of plants for purposes of propagation. (See photograph 15.) Assuming they survive (a large assumption), those cuttings will grow into diseased, bug-infested, blighted, or otherwise inferior plants. Use only healthy, robust, perfect pieces of plants for propagation.

Now that you know the "don'ts"—don't root in water, don't root in winter, don't use inferior cuttings—you're ready for the "do's" that also apply to all cuttings.

To wit: how to water cuttings. No matter what kind of cutting you take, once you place it in the rooting medium of your choice you must henceforth keep that medium uniformly moist *but (absolutely!) not soggy* up to the point where rooting begins. Exactly how you achieve this constant, uniform moisture will be determined by whether you cover or don't cover the cuttings. Placing an inflated, clear-plastic bag (or similar device) over a fledgling cutting creates high humidity. This high humidity prevents a dangerous wilt for that piece of a plant suddenly cut off from its source of water (the parent plant) and sees the cutting through this critical stage to the point where it will be able to draw water through its own new emerging roots. If you cover the cutting, you probably won't need to add any additional water to the rooting medium (until the final stages of rooting) because the plastic bag will hold in the necessary moisture. If you don't cover the cutting, the rooting medium will dry out just like any soil exposed to the air. So be sure to check it for watering every day and water often enough to keep the medium moist.

Which cuttings do you cover and which do you leave exposed to the air? It boils down to this: The *thinner* the leaf or stem or whatever of a cutting, the *faster* it will lose moisture; the *thicker* the leaf or stem or whatever of a cutting, the *more slowly* it will lose moisture.

Setting up a covered propagation pot is a cinch, but you've got to get it right. After watering the potting soil or other rooting medium, place the plant, pot and all, in a clear-plastic bag. Have a twistem or rubber band handy. Now blow air into the bag to expand the bag *away* from the cutting. Anywhere that moist bag touches the cutting, the cutting will rot. If you think you need them, stick in a few wooden stakes to hold the bag away from the cutting, then blow in air, gather the bag at the top, and seal it with the twistem or rubber band. Be sure to check the plastic bag for excessive moisture. If droplets of water form on the inside of the bag or if you feel it's too moist in there, open the bag for a few hours to let it dry out. After about four weeks or so, if your cutting is doing just fine, it will be time to deliberately open the bag for several hours a day. This way you gradually accustom your maturing cutting to the normal level of humidity in the air. At the same time start letting the medium dry out more between waterings. This gradual process is called "hardening off." Then, four weeks later, simply take the bag off and leave it off. Your cutting has smoothly and successfully adjusted to the real world.

If the thickness of your cutting tells you it doesn't need a high-humidity "incubator" in order to root, the cutting still needs to have its watering hardened off when it clearly begins to root. How will you know when it clearly begins to root? By administering the following little test: Give the cutting the most gentle, feather-light tug. If that delicate tug is met with any resistance, you know that roots have begun to anchor the cutting into the soil. If the thought of even the most light-handed tug on a cutting makes you squeamish, let us offer the following hands-off, fright-free, sure-fire, telltale sign: Because no cutting can initiate growth without roots, *where there is growth there must be roots!*

If there is growth fertilizing must commence! How do you do it? You use the theory and techniques you learned in chapter 6 on fertilizing, and do the following: Put just enough (a pinch, two pinches) powdered water-soluble fertilizer in your watering can, enough to barely tint the water. Use this highly diluted solution each and every time you water the cutting until the fall, which is the end of the growing season. Lest there be the slightest confusion, lest you think that eight tablespoons would be even better than a pinch, forget it! "More" is *not* more for your progressing cutting. *"More" will kill it.* The key phrase here is *highly diluted.* (In the case of succulent cuttings, no fertilizer whatsoever is applied until the following spring and summer.)

Next, as you already learned in chapter 8 on pruning, if your cutting came off a branching plant, now is the time to prune off its growing tip to ensure that it branches out like its parent. Why does this pruning promote branching? As chapter 8 also explains, contained in the very tips of the stems of branching plants are auxins (hormones) that inhibit branching. When you snip off these tips containing the hormones, branching jumps into action on the remaining length of the stem. And remember: Just taking off the top leaves doesn't do the trick. You must get the stem.

Now that you have the general do's and don'ts of propagation under your belt, you're ready to explore the various techniques. Nature has devised a myriad of ways for plants to multiply and be bountiful. As indoor plant hobbyists, our pleasant task is first to understand and then to manipulate this ingenious bounty to our own purposes. We are well aware that neither your needs nor your interests include propagative techniques such as sweating out long minutes at a kitchen table trying to perform "leaf sectioning" on a begonia leaf or waiting twelve months for the spores or seeds of a fern to grow into something vaguely resembling a little fern. So we have pared down our information to seven of the most popular (but often misunderstood) ways of making new plants from old plants: stem cuttings, one-leaf propagation, the ever-popular air layering, runners, off-sets, suckers, and division.

Stem Cuttings

We'll begin with "stem cuttings." Simply stated, a stem cutting is a piece of the stem taken off a plant that is capable of branching. These include coleus, Swedish ivies, many of the Peperomias, many of the philodendrons, all of the *Dracaenas*, and *Ficus* trees. Stem cuttings can also be taken off branching cacti and succulents. We'll get into the unique needs of these succulent cuttings after we treat foliage stem cuttings.

Whether it comes from a foliage or succulent plant, a stem cutting can be a "terminal tip cutting" that includes the terminal growing tip at the very top of the stem, or it can be a "regular" stem cutting taken from further down on the stem and not including the tip. Both will work. To better understand the difference between the two, let's pretend that a foot-long snake is a foot-long piece of stem. At the front end of the snake is the head (the terminal tip); the rest is body (or stem). If you chopped off four inches from the front end of the stem, you'd have a piece of the snake with its head. This is a "terminal tip cutting." If you chopped off the next four inches, you'd have a piece of the body. This is a "regular" stem cutting.

As you already know, you choose only perfect, flawless, healthy stems from which to take your cuttings. If the cat sat on part of your plant's foliage, you cannot take your cuttings from these squashed stems. Similarly, the fungus-blighted or bug-infested parts of your plant that chapter 8 on pruning directed you to prune off for your plant's health are not sources for cuttings. But if, as chapter 8 also states, you're about to prune back the stems of a branching plant in splendid health to promote more branching, the pieces you cut off will make splendid cuttings.

This brings us to the next question: How long should the average foliage stem cutting be? The general rule of thumb is four inches. If you had visions of lopping off ten-inch sections of stems and shoving these nice long pieces into a pot to make an instant plant, forget it! (See photograph 15.) There is no way roots could ever grow fast enough to get water up to a piece of plant that long. The cutting would simply wilt, never to recover. So don't think you can trick Mother Nature. Four inches is four inches!

How many cuttings should you put in a pot? As many as will nicely fill that pot without crowding. So go ahead and snip away.

Now the nitty-gritty: How do you take a stem cutting off your plant? It's simple. You apply the pruning principles and techniques for branching plants that you learned in chapter 8 on pruning and do the following: Go down four inches on the stem. Pinch off with your fingernails (if it's a soft stem) or cut off with a sharp scissors (if it's a hard stem) the stem right at a "node." A "node," as you may recall from chapter 8, is that juncture where a leaf is or used to be attached to a stem. With some plants, such as a *Dracaena marginata*, nodes are so close together that it hardly matters where you cut. But with a pothos plant (*Scindapsus*) where the space between nodes (called the internode) can be a good three or four inches, where you cut matters very much to the health and well-being (not to mention the appearance) of the parent plant. If you don't cut right above a node, the remaining leafless, useless, awful-looking piece of internode invites fungus and bacteria to attack it during

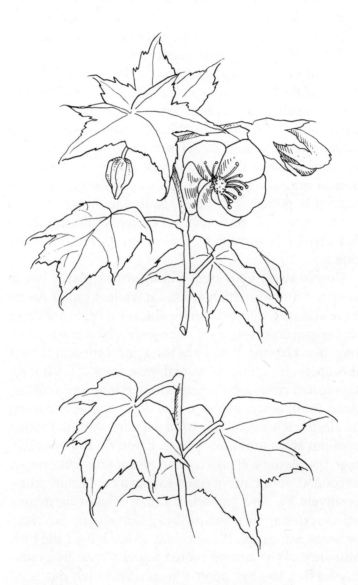

Stem cutting

those days that it shrivels up, to eventually fall off. Don't subject yourself or your plants to unnecessary trauma. Where possible, get those pinches or cuts at nodes!

Before you insert your regulation-size five-inch cuttings into the rooting medium, be sure to snip off the leaves of the bottom two or so nodes. Having done this, simply push your cuttings far enough down into the medium so that you're catching the two or so deleafed nodes *under* the medium. (The new roots will grow out of these nodes.) This setting will also have the upper sets of remaining leaves just above the soil line. Your cutting is perfectly in place. Now you water. As you already know, all cuttings must be kept uniformly moist but absolutely not soggy. Stem cuttings are no exception.

Do you cover your stem cutting with a plastic bag to keep the humidity high around it while it roots? As we have said, this depends on the thickness of the cutting's leaves and stems. If it's a thick-leafed Swedish ivy cutting, don't bother. (But do be thoughtful enough to treat this open-air cutting to several mistings a day.) If it's a thin-leafed cutting that came off something like a coleus, don't think twice, bag it! If you don't bag your cutting in plastic, it's up to you to make sure that its rooting medium stays uniformly moist. If you do bag your cutting, the plastic will take care of this for you. Either way, as soon as your cutting starts to root as indicated proof-positively by new growth, it's time to start hardening off its watering by allowing it to gradually dry out more between waterings. It's also time to harden off the high humidity of the cutting rooted under plastic by gradually leaving the bag open a longer time each day until the day you take the bag off and leave it off. This is also the time to start fertilizing using the methods and techniques outlined earlier, where you put a dash of powdered water-soluble fertilizer into your watering can. Use this highly diluted solution to water this cutting until the fall, when the active growth season is over.

Because this stem cutting came off a branching plant, now is the time to pinch or cut out the growing tip to ensure that this cutting branches out like its parent. Remember, just snipping off the top leaves does nothing; you must get the stem. (If you're worried about it, refer to chapter 8 on pruning for more details.) Approximately four weeks later, prune the growing tips of the resulting *new* stems a second time to ensure that they too branch out. Perform this ritual once a month throughout the remaining active-growth season. By the fall you will have sitting in your "propagation pot" a lush, multibranched plant that *you raised*. The following spring it will offer up its stem cuttings to the next generation of homegrown beauties. The cycle has come full circle.

How do you handle a succulent stem cutting taken from a succulent branching plant such as a jade plant (*Crassula*), a burro's tail (*Sedum*), a candelabra cactus (*Euphorbia*), and the like? You follow all the techniques and considerations you just learned for foliage stem cuttings, with the following very important exceptions:

First, where you can sometimes squeak through and get away with rooting a foliage stem cutting in water, *don't even think* about it with a succulent stem cutting. With all that water stored in its tissues, a succulent stem cutting placed in a jar of water will rot, rot, rot *every time* and turn into green mush.

Second, the base of any succulent stem cutting must be given the necessary time to heal and form a "callus" where it was severed from the mother plant. This must be done *before* you insert it in the rooting medium. This drying-out time may be a matter of hours for small pieces or as long as days and weeks for thicker pieces. There's no rushing here. It takes as long as it takes. If you skip this critical step and shove the cutting with its open wound into a rooting medium, it will rot! So place the cutting on a shelf to dry in the open air and play the waiting game. Don't worry that the cutting will wilt. It's got plenty of stored water in its tissues to sustain it while its base heals. Worry that in the wait you may forget about it altogether!

Third, because the tissues of succulent stem cuttings can easily subsist on the water already stored in them while they wait to root, you are allowed to exceed the four-inch length prescribed for foliage stem cuttings. But do be reasonable. This doesn't mean that you can shove two-foot-long pieces into a pot to create an instant desert scene! It means you aren't restricted to four inches but can go for five inches, or six inches, or even eight inches in some cases. We caution you, however, that as you get into longer succulent cuttings, they weigh more and it becomes more and more difficult to anchor them firmly in the rooting medium. Any cutting that wobbles around because it's too big or too heavy will refuse to root!

Fourth, the "uniformly moist but (absolutely!) not soggy" dictum that tells you how to water all rooting cuttings is even more important for succulent cuttings. If "moist" even dares to become "soggy," your cutting will rot! (When the cutting starts to root, again harden off your watering to let the medium dry out longer between waterings.)

Fifth, if you expect a succulent stem cutting to root in the same three to four weeks that it takes a foliage stem cutting to root, you will be sorely disappointed. Just as a mature succulent plant grows much more slowly than its foliage counterpart, succulent cuttings take much much longer to root. Depending upon the size of the cutting, this can be as long as two months, three months, or even six months.

Sixth, do not cover succulent stem cuttings to keep the humidity high around them while they root. Cover them and they will rot.

Seventh, do not apply fertilizer to succulent stem cuttings after new growth tells you they have begun to root. Fertilize them and their new little succulent roots will burn! Hold off any fertilizing until the *following* spring and summer.

Last, do pinch out (or snip off) the growing tips of rooted succulent stem cuttings to make them branch just like their parents. Due to their slow rate of growth, it's doubtful they'll need more than one pinch for the first growing season that ends when fall arrives.

One-Leaf Propagation

Next on our list is one-leaf propagation. This method is employed to propagate nonbranching foliage plants whose leaves emanate from a central crown, such as African violets, gloxinias, Rex begonias, piggyback plants (*Tolmiea*), and the like. It also works for leafed succulents whose special needs we'll treat later.

Let's look at an African violet (*Saintpaulia*) to see how

One-leaf propagation

to take a leaf cutting. As you learned in chapter 8 in the section on how to prune a leaf off a crowning plant, you carefully snip off a leaf's stem right where the stem is attached to the parent plant. Now snip another two inches off this stem. The result is a "leaf cutting," a leaf with two or so inches of stem. How many leaves do you root in a pot? Because the crowning shape of a mature African violet (and other crowning plants) will occupy the entire pot, the general rule of thumb is one leaf per pot. Gently but firmly slide the stem into the medium on an angle, pushing it far enough in so that the base of the leaf just makes contact with the soil. With time, the old leaf decomposes and a new violet grows.

How do you water this leaf cutting? You water it the same as any other cutting—enough to keep the rooting medium uniformly moist but (absolutely!) not soggy. Like any other cutting, when new growth tells you it has started to root, start hardening off by letting the soil dry out longer between waterings.

Do you cover this African violet leaf in plastic to keep high humidity around it while it roots? Some avid violet propagators would say no question about it, bag it! Others would say no, the leaf is thick enough to do just fine in the open air. So you decide. If your open-air leaf starts to wilt or fail in any way, get a bag on it pronto. (If, by the way, your leaf cutting comes from a thin-leafed piggyback plant that wilts at the drop of a hat even when it's attached to its parent, you should be ready with the plastic bag when inserting the leaf into the rooting medium!)

If you've forgotten what you learned earlier about the growth structure of crowning plants, let us remind you again that your maturing leaf cutting will never need pinching out of its growing tips because it hasn't got any in the first place. The only pruning you will ever do to this cutting is to snip off a leaf if it yellows or is damaged in any way. While you're spared the pruning of growing tips, you're not spared fertilizing. In fact, you're eager to do it because you want to help your fast-maturing cutting make the most of its first growing season. So as soon as those new leaves start to grow, start fertilizing with the technique that applies to all cuttings—where you add a pinch of powdered water-soluble fertilizer to your watering can. You use this highly diluted solution to fertilize (and water) your cutting until the fall, when the growing season is over.

How do you propagate a succulent leaf cutting from a leafed succulent such as a jade plant (*Crassula*), a burro's tail (*Sedum*), a Kalanchoe, a snake plant (*Sansevieria*), and the like? It's easy. Twist, pinch, or snip off a leaf. Place the leaf anywhere in the open air for a few hours so that its base can dry and form a callus. Then, detached-end first, insert the leaf on an angle far enough into a rooting medium so that the base of the leaf is just under the medium. From the base of the leaf, roots will grow down and a new plant will grow up. Place as many succulent leaf cuttings as will comfortably fit in a pot, then follow *each and every step* outlined earlier for succulent stem cuttings. And you're on your way to a potful of new succulents!

Air Layering

Now we get to the area of propagation that seems to invoke fascination (and more problems) than any other— the technique known as "air layering." Air layering amounts to a sophisticated stem cutting. It is a method of propagation employed on mature (larger than a two-inch diameter), hard, fibrous trunks of branching foliage plants such as *Ficus* trees, *Dracaenas*, camellias, hibiscus, and *Pleomeles*. It enables you to take large cuttings of two- and three-foot lengths. Otherwise, these would not be possible because the procedure develops a working root system on the cutting *before* it is detached from the parent plant. If you lopped off and planted large sections of a plant without first doing this procedure, these large sections, with no roots to draw water, would wilt, keel over, and die!

Here's how to do it: First, make sure you have a packet of "rooting hormone" powder handy. (You can buy it in any plant shop or garden center.) Next, eyeball the plant. You're looking for a healthy, robust, one- or two-foot terminal piece of trunk. A "terminal" piece, as you recall from the discussion of stem cuttings, is a piece of a stem that includes the growing tip at the very top of the stem. Having chosen the desirable piece, plan on cutting about five inches below the last leaf on the desired section of trunk. If there happen to be leaves at the point where you want to cut, remove them; for, say, a two-foot piece of terminal trunk, you should get about eight inches of bare stem. Now, holding a sharp knife firmly in hand, cut *up* into the trunk about one-third of the way. Don't panic at this point and lose your nerve or momentum. If you cut in less, the trunk will know that you're just fooling around and will eventually heal itself. Your jangled nerves will have been for naught. So *cut!*

Air layering
Step 1

Take a small chip of wood or a wooden toothpick and, quickly, jam it up into the incision to keep it open. Without inhaling the stuff yourself, dust the open incision with some rooting hormone. Next, take a good wad of long-haired sphagnum moss, which is sold at any good plant shop or garden center. After it is wet and carefully wrung out, jam it into the open incision. Grab some more moist moss and make a snug fitting collar all around the trunk, going up four inches above and four inches below the point of incision. Press firmly on this moss with your fingers and palms to make sure it stays put against the trunk. Enclose the whole moss-wrapped area with a piece of clear plastic, sealing the bottom and top with a twistem. You've done it! Surgery is over.

In the weeks and months to come, a whole new root system will grow out of that incision. All you have to do to help it along is to make sure that the moss never dries out. How will you know? It will lighten in color. If this happens, open the top twistem, pour in a little water, and reseal it.

When lots of roots are clearly visible through the plastic, the good news is that Independence Day is upon

Step 2

you. Get the following few steps right, and the procedure will be a complete success.

Take off the plastic but leave the moss on. Go down three inches from the base of the moss and chop! (Don't forget to prune the parent plant's trunk back to the next node.) Place some all-purpose potting soil at the bottom of a clay pot (*not* a lightweight plastic pot). Place your cutting into the soil so that, when you're through, the soil will just cover the top of the sphagnum moss. Now water. End of procedure.

Keep this air-layered cutting uniformly moist but (absolutely!) not soggy for a few weeks, then start to harden off by letting the soil dry out further between waterings. Cut off this cutting's growing tip to get branching going, and start the highly diluted water-soluble fertilizings until the fall.

Can you air-layer succulent plants? No way! This method of propagation is strictly for foliage plants.

Step 3

Runners

We come now to "runners," "offsets," and "suckers." "Runners" are shoots that produce a little plant identical to the parent at their tips. Runners can be thin and stringy like those that dangle off Boston ferns and strawberry begonias (*Saxifraga*), or they can be thick and sturdy like those that arch off the common spider plant (*Chlorophytum*).

Runners are handled in two ways. If the plantlet at the tip of a runner has already grown a number of leaves and is sprouting roots (as a spider plantlet will do), this "baby" is ready to have its umbilical cord cut. Cleanly snip off that cord right where it attaches to the "baby," then follow through and snip the cord where it attaches to the mother plant. Pot the cutting in its own little pot, making sure that the cutting is firmly anchored in the soil and that all its roots are covered.

The stringy, fragile runners produced by ferns and strawberry begonias produce plantlets at their tips that are equally stringy and fragile. Therefore, plant these tender cuttings in their own pots while still attached to the mother plant. Only snip the "apron strings" *after* the cutting grows lots of new leaves and looks strong and sturdy.

Do you cover these cuttings to prevent moisture loss while they root? No need to! The fragile cutting still attached to the runner continues to get water from its mother while it roots. The sturdy cutting that hit the soil with roots already developed will use those roots to draw its own water supply. For the next few weeks keep the potting soil uniformly moist but (absolutely!) not soggy, then start hardening off the waterings. At

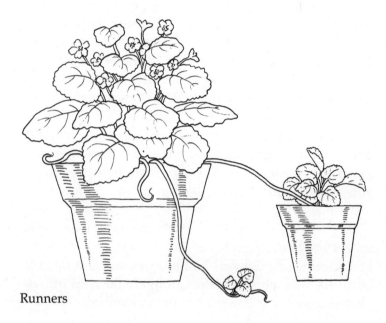

Runners

the same time, start your highly diluted fertilizing regime and continue until the fall.

Do you prune off the growing tips of these cuttings?
You can't, because there aren't any. Like their parents,
these cuttings have nonpinchable central crowns.

Offsets

Succulents don't produce runners, but not to worry,
succulents grow "offsets." "Offsets" are plantlets that
grow very close to the base of succulent plants such as
the "medicine plant" (*Aloe vera*), snake plants (*Sansevieria*), gasterias, and haworthias. Wait for offsets to grow
to a manageable size (why pick on a baby?) before you

carefully cut them off. Like tadpoles, offsets are on their own once hatched and detached. Because these are succulent cuttings, you wait the necessary hours or days for a callus to form on the base of the offset where it was attached to the mother plant. Then insert this plantlet into the rooting medium of your choice, making sure it's firmly anchored.

How do you water offsets? Like any other cutting, you water them enough to keep their medium uniformly moist but (absolutely!) not soggy, until new growth begins, when you start hardening off the frequency of waterings.

Do you cover succulent offsets in plastic bags? Not unless you want them to rot! Do you fertilize offsets the first spring and summer? Not unless you want them to burn! As with all succulent cuttings, you hold off fertilizing until the following spring and summer.

Offset

Sucker

Suckers

"Suckers" are plantlets that grow out from the base of the parent plant. They occur only on foliage plants. Staghorn ferns (*Platycerium*) make suckers and so do all the bromeliads. You allow suckers to grow to a manageable size while still attached to the parent plant before you send them out into the world alone. When the day comes, go right in there with clippers or a sharp knife and cut right where the sucker's stem is attached to the parent. Now pot it in a good potting soil, making sure to firmly anchor it so it won't wobble. Water the soil and continue to keep it uniformly moist but (absolutely!) not soggy until new growth starts.

Do you cover suckers in plastic bags to keep the humidity high around them while they root? Generally speaking, it's a good idea. When new growth signals that roots are beginning to sprout, start hardening off the high humidity in the bag by keeping it open for longer periods each day. At the same time, start hardening off the uniformly moist soil by letting it dry out somewhat between waterings. At the same time, start fertilizing by adding a pinch of powdered water-soluble fertilizer to the water in your watering can. Stop fertilizing when the growing season is over in the fall.

By the way, you don't pinch the growing tips off suckers because they don't have any!

Division

Let's turn now to "division," that age-old method of propagation. It was resorted to when our grandmothers—who instinctively knew what they were doing—lugged that gigantic twenty-five-year-old tub stuffed and overflowing with snake plants to the kitchen table, wrestled the thing out of its pot, and promptly chopped it in half with a kitchen cleaver. That's pretty much what we do today to divide in halves or thirds plants such as asparagus ferns, aspidistras, Boston ferns, palm trees, and bamboo plants.

Lest you think that "teasing" apart or somehow pulling away at the desired sections of the plant with your fingers is kinder to the plant, forget it! That misplaced sentiment will wreak havoc with the roots. A good chop or clean slice does far less damage. So do it! All it requires is a set mind and a good steady hand directing a good slice or chop through that rootball. And there

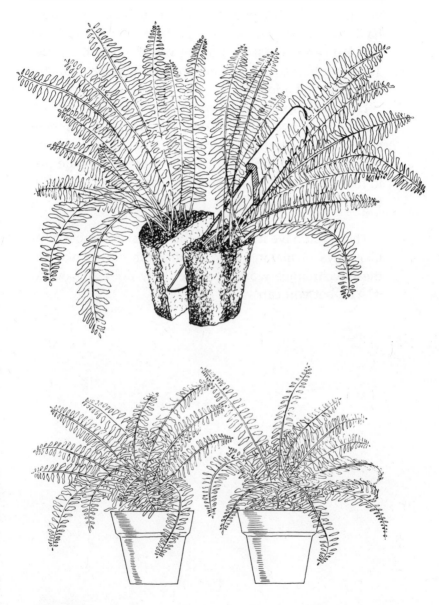

Division

you have it! Where before you had one plant, you now have two! One piece goes right back into the original pot. Add the necessary potting soil to fill in the gaps. The other half goes into a new pot of the same diameter with new soil added.

Do you alter your usual watering technique to accommodate these two "new" plants? Not necessarily. Is there any reason to withhold fertilizer? None at all, as long as your water-soluble fertilizer is diluted to a pale tint in the water. Do you prune back these plants to induce branching? No way! These plants don't branch.

There you have it! Seven of the easiest and most popular ways of making new plants from old plants. Do these techniques work? You bet they do! Can you do it? You bet you can!

10.

How <u>Not</u> to Pay Big Money for a Big Mistake

or The Right Way to Choose Large Floor Plants for Your Home and Office

Why do we allot a special chapter to floor plants? Don't the same rules and regulations that govern the selection of small- and medium-sized plants apply to green giants headed for the ceiling? Answer: They most certainly do! Furthermore, everything else you learned in previous chapters—how to water, how to put together a proper potting soil, how to transplant, how to get rid of bugs, how to prune, how to fertilize, how to propagate—also applies to large floor plants. The only difference (which starts with how much you pay for them!) between large plants and small plants is a quantitative one—the difference between large and small.

This difference *quantitatively* affects some aspects of the care of large plants. At transplant time, it translates into making up *more* potting soil than you'd need for a smaller plant. It translates into running out of fertilizer sooner rather than later because there's *more* plant to fertilize. These quantitative differences are benign enough, but they impact with serious results when it comes to watering large plants. How so? In chapter 3 on how to water plants, you learned that all plants, big, small, and anything in between, must dry out between thorough waterings. While it certainly will take more water to thoroughly soak the soil of a large plant than a small plant, you will water the large plant *far less often:* That is, while a small plant might take a week to dry out, a large plant might take a month. Or two months!

So what approach do you take? Review chapter 3 on watering. Read about the signs a plant sends out when it's thirsty. Pay particular attention to the methods used to thoroughly water a plant. Then be sure to heed that bit of advice especially tailored for nervous types: Go to the nearest plant shop and buy yourself a "moisture meter." This wonderful, inexpensive little gadget has a gauge on its head that reads 1 to 10. When the gauge reads "dry" (between 1 and 3), it's time to water your floor plant. Will this moisture meter take the worry out of the long waits between waterings, particularly if it's your first big floor plant? You bet it will! Use it.

The quantitative differences between large plants and small plants continue to operate when something goes wrong. For instance, when a $10 coleus plant that belongs in the sun is relegated to a dark corner, it falls apart in a week and dies a yellow death. The heartache most certainly is there, but if we can get mercenary and talk dollars and cents, contrast the heartache over the $10 coleus to the misery of the guy who emptied his wallet of *ten* ten-dollar bills to buy the tree-sized croton that kicks the bucket in the dark because it too needed the full sun. And this croton doesn't "check out" in one swift week like the small coleus. This big croton takes *eight* weeks to completely fall apart and die.

What's the moral of the story? When things go wrong with big plants that cost more, the misery you suffer is not only bigger, it lasts longer! But why pay big money for a big (prolonged!) mistake when, just as easily, you can choose the right plant for your home or office that starts off big and stays that way! And continues to deliver big enjoyment and big beauty in the years to come! What's the right floor plant for the money? Budget aside (that's strictly your business), the choice is dictated by your ability to meet a plant's needs (as you already learned in chapter 2 on how to choose plants). What's the first and most important consideration? *Light.* If you've got Full Sun or Moderate Light, the list of candidates to choose from is long. If you've only got Shade, the list is a little shorter. But either way, be assured that there's a floor plant out there for you that will put that final, wonderful finishing touch on an otherwise perfectly nice but "lifeless" home interior, or that will brighten up and make more humane an orderly but drab office.

The first point we want to make perfectly clear is that *there is large indoor green life beyond a* Ficus *tree!* Our intention is hardly to cast aspersions on that queen of indoor trees, the small-leafed *Ficus,* whose delicate, green foliage arches over so many couches in so many living rooms and whose presence gratefully softens the straight edges of so many office lobbies across our land. Our point is simply that contrary to what you have correctly observed, the *Ficus* tree, beauty that she be, is not the first and last word on large indoor greenery. Would you believe there are other large plants to choose from? Therefore, rather than start out with the lovely *Ficus* tree song that plays over and over in so many heads, let's see if we can't register some new melodies.

What new melodies do we have to offer? Each and every one of the floor plants that follows. As you'll soon see, our aim in this sampling is not just to make sure you don't overlook those sturdy *Dracaenas* and reliable palms. We also want to acquaint you with a few of the more exotic floor plants you always shied away from because you assumed the exotic look translated to exotic care. As you'll discover, the requirements of some of these not-so-ordinary beauties can be quite ordinary! To make it easy for you to choose which trees are right for your decor and your light, we list, in descending order of brightness, trees for Sun, trees for Moderate Light, trees for Moderate-to-Dim Light, and then trees for downright Dim Light.

Is your office or living room blasted with full sun fourteen hours a day that makes everything and everyone wilt? Then go with that sun and create a real tropical look that will give everyone a lift. Bring in a dwarf banana tree (*Musa nana*). A dwarf banana reaches five to six feet at maturity and looks as though it was lifted from a Florida backyard. It loves and thrives in all that sun. One year it will delight everyone by actually producing a little clump of small, edible bananas!

Okay, you say, we've got the sun, but it gets cool and downright cold in the office and in the garden room in the winter months. What do you have for us? Would you believe a flowering camellia (*Camellia japonica*)? This is a deep green, glossy-leafed tree that produces dazzling flowers in the spring and summer months. But it must have that cool winter temperature to thrive. Are there any restrictions? Though the flowering camellia is easy to care for, you must regularly spray-mist or use a humidifier to get all those flower buds to open. The show is well worth the effort. At flower time you'll think you're living or working in Paradise!

Dwarf banana
(*Musa nana*)

Flowering camellia
(*Camellia japonica*)

Along the same lines—bright light, cool temperatures, high humidity at blooming time—think about trying a hibiscus (*Hibiscus rosa-sinensis*). This tree produces splendid flowers that last only one day. But the flowers come in a myriad of colors and bloom in a succession day after day and can do so all summer long. As though such blossoms weren't enough, the tree is also available in a variety with cream-and-white variegation in its leaves. Talk about breathtaking!

Are flowers "too pretty" and frivolous for the look of your brightly lit home or office, but you still have to deal with a cool-to-cold winter temperature? Then try a *Pittosporum tobira*. This densely foliated plant comes in plain green and varieties with white variegation in the leaves. It couldn't be happier with the chilly winter days, and it's extremely sturdy. It makes you feel as though you had an outdoor shrub living indoors with you.

Is your home or office bright with lots of sun but its interior is a bit on the drab side? Then go for colorful crotons. These plants, readily available in tree size, come in all the colors of the rainbow. The brighter the light, the more intense the colors will be! And, like a green lawn suddenly graced with peacocks, your dull surroundings will jump to life.

Do you want more "peacocks" to choose from for your brightly lit but dull interiors? The *Dracaena marginata* now comes in a 'Tricolor' variety. Its leaves sport pale green, cream, white, pink—all the way to red! Grow this one in blazing sun and you will have a study in vibrant pastels. It's unbelievable. Similarly, the Song of India (*Pleomele reflexa variegata*) is now available in a spectacular green-and-white-leafed variety. It's every bit as sturdy as the plain green *Pleomele* if you've got the good light!

Flowering hibiscus
(Hibiscus rosa-sinensis)

Pittosporum tobira

Does the look of a bamboo plant (*Phyllostachys aurea*) appeal to your sense of the exotic? Then, if you have terrific light, why not consider one of these for your home or office? While they do have that "Casablanca" look, they also have a tendency to occasionally shed a few leaves, so there is some maintenance involved, however slight.

Is your work or living area very bright, very straight-angled, and very modern? Do you want plants that will conform to the bold, clean lines? Then go all out for tall upright cacti. They virtually take care of themselves and will be pieces of living sculpture.

Do you want a little more variety of shape than a straight-up-and-down cactus affords but still want to avoid the look and maintenance of "leafy" plants? Then choose sun-loving succulents such as the candelabra cactus (*Euphorbia lactae*) or pencil cactus (*Euphorbia tirucalli*). These succulents still have the clean lines to match your decor, but they branch out freely and give you a variety of shapes and textures to work with. A collection of these plants can be spectacular, and just like cacti, these succulents are virtually care-free.

Do you want to go in the opposite direction and get leafy? Then look into a false aralia (*Dizygotheca elegantissima*). Grown in the preferred full sun, this plant's delicate-looking leaves take on a purple hue. Grown in moderate light, the leaves stay green. Either way, this plant's graceful foliage makes it a winner. One word of caution: The scale insect (see chapter 7) is very fond of this plant, so be sure to carefully examine the stems and leaves of any candidate at your local plant shop or nursery before purchasing.

Bamboo
*(Phyllostachys
aurea)*

Pencil cactus
(Euphorbia tirucalli)

False aralia
(Dizygotheca elegantissima)

Podocarpus
macrophyllus
'Maki'

Is your light moderately bright? Then try a *Podocarpus macrophyllus* 'Maki.' Why this graceful, tall beauty that looks like a delicate indoor evergreen rarely makes the pages of the plant books is a mystery to us. It's a smashing floor plant. It comes in both an upright and "weeping over" variety, and it's sturdy, sturdy, sturdy.

Is your moderately bright interior crying for lots of big, leafy plants? Then rely on that great old standby, the Schefflera. Its leaves are big and green and bold and glossy. It will give you a cool, wonderful, tropical look.

What other plants will do well in Moderate Light? Fortunately, you have all the palm trees to choose from. But do not feel that you're restricted to the nice but ubiquitous green-leaves-with-yellow-tinges areca palm. This tree has become the *Ficus* tree of the indoor palm world! Don't overlook the areca, but make sure you also consider the resilient bamboo palms (*Chamaedorea*), which look like a cross between an areca palm and a bamboo plant. Then there's the expensive but exceptional lady palm (*Rhapis*) and the costly but beautiful Kentia palm.

Which floor plants do well in Moderate-to-Dim Light? Except for the aforementioned sun-loving *Dracaena marginata* 'Tricolor,' you have all the rest of the sturdy *Dracaenas* to choose from. There's the corn plant (*Dracaena fragrans massangeana*) with the yellow band that runs down each broad leaf. There's the striped *Dracaena* (*Dracaena deremensis* 'Warneckii') that has green-and-white-striped leaves. Don't overlook the very sturdy plain green *Dracaena* 'Janet Craig.' Then too you have several varieties of large philodendrons to choose from. Some of these plants will need staking to hold them upright; others are self-heading, that is, they hold themselves up. One of the loveliest of the self-heading kinds is the

Song of India
(Pleomele reflexa variegata)

finger philodendron (*Philodendron selloum*). This plant produces arching stems that end in a graceful spread of "finger" leaves.

What other floor plant can you place in Moderate-to-Dim Light? Do you remember the aforementioned bold-leafed Schefflera for light no less than moderate? Well, fortunately, it has a cousin, the Hawaiian Schefflera (*Schefflera venulosa*) that is not so particular about its light. This Schefflera is small-leafed and very sturdy. It branches out laterally with ease and holds those branches even in dim light. With age, though, this Hawaiian Schefflera is going to need some staking to hold it upright. Not to worry: The stake will disappear in all its dense, tight foliage.

Are there floor plants that will work in dimly lit locations? You bet there are! Here are two unusual ones to choose from. Do you remember the aforementioned green-and-white-leafed Song of India (*Pleomele reflexa variegata*) that belongs strictly in bright light? It was developed from the plant we want to talk about here—the plain green *Pleomele reflexa*. It is amazing to us that this plant is not more readily available because, like the snake plant, it is virtually indestructible. Yet its look is quite exotic. Speaking of exotic looking but no fancy care needed, let's look at a ponytail palm (*Beaucarnea recurvata*). This magnificent plant produces a large, swollen base that tapers up to a slender trunk and ends in a head of foliage. The foliage is made up of long, thin, bladelike leaves that cascade down like water splashing down from a fountain. The only problem you might have with this plant is keeping your cat off it! How so? Cats love to chew on long, thin-leafed foliage. With any luck your ponytail palm is going to have lots of this kind

Ponytail palm
(Beaucarnea recurvata)

of foliage, so, if push comes to shove, you may have to choose between your wonderful cat and this wonderful plant.

Now that you have a better feel for some of the lesser-known but very worthwhile floor plants, let's return to the queen of indoor greenery that generally comes to the public's mind first—the small-leafed *Ficus* tree. Why are these trees so popular? First, they are aggressively marketed. Second, no other plant gives that special feeling of an indoor tree quite like a *Ficus*.

How and where do you grow them? At The Village Green we have a time-honored saying about these trees. We say it so often in fact that it may well become our epitaph. The saying goes like this: "The more light you have, the more leaves you'll have." A *Ficus* tree grown in full sun will be lush and green and spectacular, with foliage so dense you'll hardly be able to see through it. This tree will be a source of pure joy for you and all onlookers. A *Ficus* tree will tolerate moderately bright light and have ample leaves, but hardly as numerous or dense as the one basking in sun. A *Ficus* tree relegated to dim light will have leaves so stringy and sparse that eventually you'll be able to count them on ten fingers. Last but not least, a *Ficus* tree placed in the dark will whittle itself (and you) down to nothing. What's the moral of the story? *Light.*

There's more to the story. As truly sturdy and dependable and beautiful as these trees are, they do have this nagging tendency (not unfamiliar to the masses of you so afflicted) to sometimes enter into a most unfortunate condition popularly referred to as shock. What is shock? It is your *Ficus* tree's way of saying that it is in distress. How will you know? It's unmistakable! Apart from the normal attrition rate whereby a few leaves yellow and fall off, shock is indicated by lots of yellow leaves—*loads* of yellow leaves—that plink down onto the floor in a daily cascade. You anxiously sweep them up at night and bingo! the next morning there's a whole fresh bunch on the floor to torture you. You accidentally brush past the tree—or, God forbid, you sneeze nearby—and down come more handfuls! With each and every depressing day you watch your once luscious tree reduced to this stringy, twiggy, brown skeleton. The bulk of its lower leaves are gone and just a few green leaves at the growing tips of branches remain. Now depression turns to a feeling of impending disaster. (See photograph 16.)

What causes shock? Several things. The lesser causes include rough handling, when these trees are needlessly and pointlessly thrown around at delivery time as though they were lifeless totem poles. Then there is that culpable rough, tough treatment at transplant time that can sometimes send an otherwise perfectly healthy specimen plummeting into shock. And there's the case of the tree whose soil the family kitty habitually mistakes for its litter box. Let's not forget the overly happy party guest whose mug of beer spills into the *Ficus* tree's pot. None of these events is particularly appreciated by your *Ficus* tree, but the main cause of shock for nine out of ten trees is none of the above. The number-one culprit is *overwatering!* As chapter 3 stresses, this means watering too soon. So whether that *Ficus* tree is basking in the preferred full sun, nicely resigned to the moderate light, or just barely hanging in there in the lower light, like the rest of our floor plants its soil must dry out between thorough waterings. What happens if it doesn't dry out? This is what happens: X amount of roots will rot and die. Those leaves cut off from their life-giving water supply will yellow, die, and fall off. Your *Ficus* tree is now in shock.

What's the number-two cause of shock? *Skimpy waterings*. What does skimpy mean? It means sprinkling a little water here, a little water there. It means underwatering or not watering all the soil thoroughly when you water. (See chapter 3 on watering.) This means that even if the intervals between waterings are indeed correct, shock can still result if all that soil is not thoroughly saturated at watering time. Why? Those roots (which will eventually shrivel up and die) that are not receiving water cannot get water up to thirsty leaves. Back to square one: Leaves deprived of water yellow, die, and fall off, and shock results.

So *over*watering (too soon) and *under*watering (not enough) are the two main culprits for *Ficus* tree "shock." We assure you that either one is serious enough to do the trick. But commit both mistakes (watering in small amounts too soon)—which is usually the case—and you'd better keep the broom, dustpan, and a box of tissues handy. You're gonna need them!

There's more to this tale of woe. Once triggered, shock can easily get out of control. Emergency lights flashing, the distressed tree sheds the leaves connected to the dead roots all right, but with wheels set in motion and adrenaline pumping, the tree overreacts and continues to shed leaves and more leaves and more leaves. The shock has gained momentum. The emergency system has gone haywire.

Is there anything you can do to control shock, to stop it before it swallows your plant in a mountain of yellow leaves? We're happy to say that there are several things you can do. The first is, *don't panic!* It's counterproductive. All is not quite as bleak as it looks. In a very real sense, particularly in the early stages, the condition of shock is very much a lifesaving mechanism. How so? If you recall, chapter 3 on watering says that all plants maintain a proportion of so many leaves to so many roots. You may also recall that if those roots are disturbed for any reason(s), the plant will eliminate the necessary foliage in order to maintain the critical roots-to-leaves ratio. So the *Ficus* tree that sheds leaves in reaction to, say, overwatering is doing the only thing that it can do to save itself.

How can you prevent the process from escalating and taking over? Except for prevention, there are no guarantees, but you can put the odds very much in your favor if you *don't* do the following: First, for goodness' sake, don't continue the overwatering. If it was skimpy waterings that got you in this fix, saturate that soil *now*. As the shock runs its course and your tree continues to shed more and more leaves, you *must* adjust the frequency of waterings accordingly. To be brutally honest, as your tree continues to eliminate leaves, you have less and less of a tree. Therefore, you must not water at the same frequency you became accustomed to when all those leaves were there because, for the moment, they're not! With fewer and fewer leaves to use that water, and with less evaporation from their upper and lower surfaces, the soil is going to stay wet a whole lot longer than before. So *widen* those intervals between waterings. Conversely, as new leaves grow back, be prepared to go in the other direction and shorten those intervals. Does this feel too much like a hit-and-miss guessing game with high stakes? It isn't really, because your eye surveying the number of leaves going in one direction or the other will easily guide your hand on the watering can.

If your nerves are already shot, if one more doubt about the appropriate watering for the *Ficus* tree is going to do you in, do yourself a favor: Go out and buy one of those sure-fire 100-percent-accurate moisture meters that we talked about earlier. When the gauge at the top of the meter reads "dry" (between 1 and 3) it's time to water your tree. Long after this bout with shock is ancient history, feel free to continue letting that meter guide you.

Next on our list of what not to do: *Don't fertilize!* (See chapter 6 on fertilizing.) Your shaky tree has all it can handle now just trying to stabilize itself. A misguided dose of fertilizer at this point will be a first-class ticket to the hereafter. When can you fertilize? Assuming the calendar reads anywhere in the spring and summer months (March through October), when *Ficus* trees and all plants are actively growing, you can start or resume fertilizing when new leaves start to make an appearance. New leaves herald the end of the shock and the beginning of new life.

Remember: Whether you sweep up fallen leaves off the floor is your concern, but do *not* let them accumulate on the soil's surface. Apart from creating a dandy hiding and breeding place for bugs, that layer of dead leaves will slow down the rate of evaporation from the soil's surface. In no way do you want to interfere or tamper with that process, so remove those leaves!

We now come to a "do." That is, assuming once again that the calendar reads anywhere in the spring and summer months, *do* prune back the growing tips of branches of your *Ficus* tree in shock. At the moment you have a tree that has let go of its older leaves closer to the soil and retained leaves on its upper sections. To get this tree to branch out, leaf out, and green up the lower blank areas, you must prune off its growing tips. Another way of saying this is, if you want to get back to that wonderful leaves-all-over look that your tree had before disaster struck, get out those pruning shears and use them! How much do you prune off? As you learned in chapter 8 on pruning, the choice is up to you. Two inches will do the trick, or you can prune off more. While you're at it, be sure to remove any dead twigs that succumbed to the shock.

What else can you do to ease an ailing tree out of shock as soon as possible? Spray-mist as often as possible. Ten, twenty times a day isn't too much. That high humidity will greatly benefit the old leaves that are trying to hang on and the newcomers that are trying to emerge.

Also, if there's anything you can do to improve the quality of light available to this plant, do it. If it means moving it to the full sun it really, really wanted all along, now's the time to give it a break. If moderate or dim light is all you have, hook up some artificial light.

Last, if you're fortunate enough to have a garden and it's spring or summer, don't wait another minute to (carefully!) get that tree outside into "speckled" sun or bright shade. Why the rush? Giving your upset *Ficus* tree a few weeks in the great outdoors is like sending it to the Bahamas for a vacation. The bright light is there. The high humidity is there. There's a nice drop in temperature at night. The air circulation is terrific. All of this will make your grateful tree think it's back where it came from—the tropics. Here's more good news for you: The tree's recovery time from the shock will be about twenty times faster than the tree that recuperates indoors.

What's the best time (if there is such a thing!) for a *Ficus* tree to go into shock? Sometime during the spring and summer months, preferably the early spring. Your tree will have that active growth season so it can grow back the foliage it lost and then continue growing. What's the worst time for shock to strike? The dormant, no-growth, inactive winter months. You and your tree will more or less be stuck with each other in its current denuded state until February or March, when it will start growing back those leaves and looking like a tree again.

What's the final word on shock? When it's over, it's over. This can be a matter of days, weeks, and often months. During shock a tree can lose one-third of its leaves, half of its leaves, three-fourths of its leaves, 90 percent of its leaves, and *still come back*. Take those steps you can to minimize the effects and speed up recovery. You've done your best. The rest is up to the particular tree. Is the general prognosis good? The happy fact is that it is. As disturbing and "shocking" as the experience is, there's no reason to lose a tree from shock. Yes, it takes time. It may require some tender loving care for a while, but nine and a half out of ten trees bounce back to lead a full, productive, leafy life.

Before we leave the *Ficus* genus of trees, we first want to emphasize that only the small-leafed varieties such as *Ficus benjamina, Ficus exotica,* and *Ficus nitida* are subject to shock. Second, small-leafed fig trees are only a few members of this wonderful group of trees. There's also the big, dependable, sturdy rubber tree (*Ficus elastica*). While it prefers bright light, it does remarkably well in a lot less. This tree also comes in several varieties with cream and white and yellow in their leaves, which do require bright light. Then there's the beautiful burgundy rubber tree, whose leaves turn a deep purple in full sun.

So there you have it . . . a quick tour through the wonderful land of these remarkable, gentle indoor green giants referred to as floor plants. Some of them are green, others are colorful. Some have big, bold, splashy leaves, others are gracefully delicate. Some delight with flowers, others are strictly for the foliage. Some like it cool, others like it hot. But whatever they do and whatever they want, they're there for the choosing. Choose the right one for you and you won't bring home a big mistake. You'll bring a big burst of life into your home or office.

Index